# A
# West Country
# Christmas

Compiled by Chris Smith

ALAN SUTTON

ALAN SUTTON PUBLISHING LIMITED
BRUNSWICK ROAD · GLOUCESTER · UK

ALAN SUTTON PUBLISHING INC.
WOLFEBORO FALLS · NH 03896-0848 · USA

First published 1989

British Library Cataloguing in Publication Data

A West Country Christmas.
1. English literature. Special subjects:
Christmas – Anthologies
I. Smith, Chris
820.8,033

ISBN 0-86299-640-6

Library of Congress Cataloging in Publication Data
applied for

*Cover illustration: Christmas Archives, Cardiff.*

This book is dedicated to my mother who can't share any
of this. Particularly at Christmas time we'll miss you.

Typesetting and origination by
Alan Sutton Publishing Limited.
Printed in Great Britain by
Dotesios Printers Limited.

# A Christmas Carol

## SAMUEL TAYLOR COLERIDGE

*The singing of Christmas carols is very much part of any traditional Christmas celebration, and this is Samuel Taylor Coleridge's way of introducing us to A West Country Christmas. Coleridge was born in 1773 within a few miles of Exeter, in the small East Devon town of Ottery St Mary. The town itself is well known throughout the West Country for staging the burning of the tar barrels in November – a truly terrifying spectacle, when flaming tar barrels are carried shoulder-high through the town, a throw back to the pagan warding off of evil spirits, while ensuring good luck in the year to come – and for its beautiful parish church, a replica of Exeter's majestic cathedral. This poem sums up for me the simple nature of the Christmas story with a real feeling of reverence and awe.*

The Shepherds went their hasty way,
And found the lowly stable-shed
Where the Virgin Mother lay:
And now they checked their eager tread,
For to the Babe, that at her bosom clung
A mother's song the Virgin Mother sung.

They told her how a glorious light,
Streaming from a heavenly throng,

# · *A West Country Christmas* ·

Around them shone, suspending night!
While sweeter than a mother's song,
Blest Angels heralded the Saviour's birth,
Glory to God on high! and Peace on Earth.


She listened to the tale divine,
And closer still the Babe she prest;
And while she cried, the Babe is mine!
The milk rushed faster to her breast:
Joy rose within her, like a summer's morn;
Peace, Peace on Earth! The Prince of Peace is born.


Thou mother of the Prince of Peace,
Poor, simple and of low estate!
That strife should vanish, battle cease,
O why should this thy soul elate?
Sweet music's loudest note, the poet's story –
Didst thou ne'er love to hear of fame and glory?


And is not War a youthful king
A stately hero clad in mail?
Beneath his footsteps laurels spring;
Him Earth's majestic monarch's hail
Their friend, their playmate! and his bold bright eye
Compels the maiden's low-confessing sigh.


'Tell his in some more courtly scene,
To maids and youths in robes of state!
I am a woman poor and mean,
And therefore is my soul elate.
War is a ruffian, all with guilt defiled,
That from their aged father tears his child!

2

# · A West Country Christmas ·

'A murderous fiend, by fiends adored,
He kills the sire and starves the son;
The husband kills, and from her board
Steals all his widow's toil had won;
Plunders God's world of beauty; rends away
All safety from the night, all comfort from the day.

'Then wisely is my soul elate
That strife should vanish, battle cease:
I'm poor and of a low estate,
The Mother of the Prince of Peace.
Joy rises in me, like a summer's morn:
Peace, Peace on Earth! The Prince of Peace is born'.

Ottery St Mary church in the snow

# Angel's Song

## CHARLES CAUSLEY

*Charles Causley was born in 1917 at Launceston in Cornwall, where he still lives today. He spent nearly thirty years teaching and is a prolific writer of children's fiction, plays and poetry. This is his simple and effective rendition of the familiar tale of Christ's birth.*

FIRST ANGEL      Fear not, shepherds, for I bring
Tidings of a new-born King –
Not in castle, not in keep,
Not in tower tall and steep;
Not in manor-house or hall,
But a humble ox's stall.

SECOND ANGEL      Underneath a standing star
And where sheep and cattle are,
In a bed of straw and hay
God's own Son is born this day.
If to Bethlehem you go,
This the truth you soon shall know.

THIRD ANGEL      And as signal and as sign,
Sure as all the stars that shine,
You shall find him, shepherds all,
And the joyful news will share
With good people everywhere.

4

A merry Christmas

SER. 606 N° 2851

5

SECOND ANGEL      Therefore, listen as we cry:

THREE ANGELS      Glory be to God on high,
                  And his gifts of love and peace
                  To his people never cease.

# Hear Ye

## NELSON OWEN

*Outside Ottery St Mary church, starting at midnight on
Christmas Eve, a bell is rung three times and the town's
night-watchman proclaims the birth of Jesus by reciting
the following verse. He also gives the time and the state of
the weather and completes the proclamation by ringing the
bell again three times. The night-watchman repeats this
ceremony at various points throughout the town, so that all
are aware of the joyous occasion.*

At the Nativity of Christ our Lord
The angels did rejoice with one accord.
Let Christians imitate them here on earth
And crown this Day with joy and pious mirth.

# The Legend of the Oxen

There are many legends, superstitions and customs world-wide concerning Christmas, and one that seems to prevail in the West Country is that of the 'beasts of the field', or cattle, paying their own special tribute to Christ at his birth. I heard only recently of a farmer, now retired, who every Christmas Eve made a point of visiting his cattle, who were housed in sheds or cubicles for the winter. He maintained that they behaved quite differently at this special time of the year. They were more at peace, being subdued and quiet, as if aware of what a joyous and very special time of the year this was. Perhaps a clue to this can be found in Charles Henry Poole's *The Customs, Superstitions and Legends of the County of Somerset* of 1877, where he records that: 'The oxen are supposed to kneel at this gladsome season, in adoration of OUR LORD, on the eve of the nativity. This tradition is not confined to England, but exists in Germany. No satisfactory reason can be given; one has been attempted, and is to the effect that in old pictures of the nativity, the cattle were represented with bended knee in the stable of Bethlehem.'

It is this legend or superstition that gave Dorset's most famous literary son, Thomas Hardy, the inspiration for his well-known and beloved poem, 'The Oxen':

# · *A West Country Christmas* ·

Christmas Eve, and twelve of the clock.
'Now they are all on their knees,'
An elder said as we sat in a flock
By the embers in hearthside ease.

We pictured the meek mild creatures where
They dwelt in their strawy pen,
Nor did it occur to one of us there
To doubt they were kneeling then.

So fair a fancy few would weave
In these years! Yet, I feel,
If someone said on Christmas Eve,
'Come; see the Oxen kneel!

'In the lonely barton by yonder coomb
Our childhood used to know.'
I should go with him in the gloom,
Hoping it might be so.

The prevalence of the legend is confirmed in Richard Pearse Chope's *The Dialect of Hartland*, published in 1891, for he writes:

It was customary on Christmas Eve or on Christmas Day, according to the locality, to give cattle, horses, sheep, pigs and also domestic and wild birds, an extra supply of food. *Cattle and other animals were believed to be resposive to the approach of the anniversary of Christ's birth* and it would be an easy corollary that they should have a share of the Christmas good things. To enable them to do this an extra supply of food has been given them by immemorial custom. Also on Christmas Day at least they had to do no work.

# · A West Country Christmas ·

John Brand in his *Popular Antiquities of Great Britain* of 1870 also recorded the

> . . . superstitious notion which prevails in West Devonshire that, at twelve o'clock at night on Christmas Eve, the oxen in their stalls are always found on their knees, as in an attitude of devotion; and that (which is still more singular) since the alteration of the style they continue to do this only on the Eve of old Christmas Day. An honest countryman, living on the edge of St Stephen's Down, near Launceston, Cornwall, informed me, October 28th, 1790, that he once, with some others, made a trial of the truth of the above, and watching several oxen in their stalls at the above time, at twelve o'clock at night, they observed the two oldest oxen only fall upon their knees, and, as he expressed it in the idiom of the country, make 'a cruel moan like Christian creatures'. I could not but with great difficulty keep my countenance: he saw, and seemed angry that I gave so little credit to his tale, and walking off in a pettish humour, seemed to 'marvel at my unbelief'.

With the Season's Greetings.

# Nativity

## STANLEY STOKES

*I came across this in a volume of poetry called* A West Country New Anthology of Contemporary Poets, *although, judging by the age of the volume in the library, the anthology is no longer new. The publishers seem to have long vanished, and I have been unable to find out anything about Stanley Stokes, but have included his poem, which I would date as Victorian, as a simple and moving version of the Christmas story.*

Magic of night
A world grown still,
Restless shepherds
Upon a hill.

A tremor of wind
The fields among,
Suddensome light,
Celestial song.

Savants three
Who had journeyed far
To fathom the portent
Of a star.

A Babe asleep
With his haloed head
Pillowed on hay
In a manger.

Soft eyed kine
Disturbed and a-stare
At the wonder astir
'Neath a lanthorn there.

# An Ode on the Birth of Our Saviour

### ROBERT HERRICK

*This is the first of two Christmas poems by Robert Herrick,*
*who lived in Devon between 1629 and 1647.*

In numbers and but these few,
I sing Thy Birth, Oh JESU!
Thou prettie Babie, borne here.
With sup'rabundant score here;

# · A West Country Christmas ·

Who for Thy Princely Port here,
Hadst for Thy Place
Of Birth, a base
Out-stable for thy Court here.

Instead of neat Inclosures
Of inter-woven Osiers;
Instead of fragrant Posies
Of Daffadils, and Roses;
Thy cradle, Kingly Stranger,
As Gospel tells,
Was nothing els,
But, here, a homely manager.

But we with Silks, (not Cruells)
With sundry precious Jewells,
And Lilly-work will dresse Thee;
And as we dispossesse thee
Of clouts, wee'l make a chamber,
Sweet Babe, for Thee,
Of Ivorie,
And plastered round with Amber.

The Jewes they did disdaine Thee,
But we will entertain Thee
With Glories to await here,
Upon Thy Princely State here,
And more for love, than pittie.
From yeere to yeere
Wee'l make Thee, here,
A Free-born of our Citie.

# In the Bleak Mid-Winter

## CHRISTINA G. ROSSETTI

*I have stretched the boundaries of the West Country to include the following carol which was written by Dante Gabriel Rossetti's sister, Christina (1830–94). Rossetti himself lived just across the Wiltshire county border from 1871 to 1874. I make no apology for including Christina's carol here, as it is the perfect introduction to the piece that follows.*

*There is also another more personal reason for including it, one of my favourite carols, in this compilation. Every year in a hamlet just outside the Devon village where I live, a man called John Somers organizes children and adults alike in doing the rounds, carol singing. It's very much a community event, well supported with about twenty-five all told visiting all the outlying farms and cottages to deliver to the best of our ability some of the best-known and best-loved carols. Then it's back to friends for mulled wine and mince pies, and Christmas really seems to have started.*

*Last year as we made our way up the path to a thatched cottage, the home of a local solicitor, 'In the Bleak Mid-Winter' was the next carol on the song sheet. Having taken our cue from the introduction played on the clarinet by John's son, Ben, we launched with great gusto into our*

*rendition. The only response we got was the barking of a dog from somewhere inside the house. As the solicitor's wife was in our party, she knew that her husband was at home. Sure enough, he was soon spotted through the window by some of the children in the group, sound asleep in a fireside armchair. It turned out that it had been the office Christmas party during the day and our local solicitor was somewhat the worse for wear as a result. The dog, however, seemed to enjoy our version of Christina Rossetti's carol!*

In the bleak mid-winter
Frosty wind made moan,
Earth stood hard as iron,
Water like a stone:
Snow had fallen, snow on snow,

# · *A West Country Christmas* ·

Snow on snow.
In the bleak mid-winter, long ago.

Our God, Heaven cannot hold him
Nor earth sustain;
Heaven and earth shall flee away
When he comes to reign:
In the bleak mid-winter
A stable-place sufficed
The Lord God almighty
Jesus Christ.

Enough for him, whom Cherabim
Worship night and day,
A breastful of milk,
And a mangerful of hay.
Enough for him, whom angels
Fall down before.
The Ox and Ass and Camel
Which adore.

Angels and Archangels
May have gathered there,
Cherubim and Seraphim
Thronged the air –
But only his mother
In her maiden bliss
Worshipped the beloved
With a kiss.

What can I give him
Poor as I am?
If I were a shepherd
I would bring a lamb;

15

If I were a wise man
I would do my part;
Yet what I can I give him?
Give my heart.

*from*

# Lorna Doone

## R.D. BLACKMORE

*From 'The Bleak Mid-Winter' of the carol to 'The Great Winter' from R.D. Blackmore's classic romance, set on Exmoor and published in 1869. Blackmore certainly had his roots firmly in the West Country and Devon, having been educated at Blundell's School in Tiverton, before going on to the aptly named Exeter College in Oxford. The chapter I have chosen paints a vivid picture of the terrible weather that can sweep across the wastes of Exmoor and the never ending struggle that the farmer has to protect his stock from the elements.*

*Shortly after I moved to Devon, we had one of those winters that farmers have nightmares about, when it snows for hours on end and strong winds whip the snow into drifts against the hedges. Sheep and animals out in the fields try to take shelter by huddling up against the hedges, with the result that they often get lost and buried in the drifts which can be many feet deep. Today, of course, modern methods can be employed to rescue stock stranded in this way, and in this particular winter the army were called in to drop hay and food by helicopter and to help farmers dig the animals out from the drifts. Even with assistance like this it can be an awe-inspiring task, for it's difficult to appreciate how much snow can be moved by howling winds during the course of a night. With this in mind, R.D. Blackmore's picture of one man's single-handed battle to protect his livelihood makes gripping reading.*

It must have snowed most wonderfully to have made that depth of covering in about eight hours. For one of Master Stickles' men, who had been out all night, said that no snow had begun to fall until nearly midnight. And here it was blocking up the doors, stopping the ways, and the water-courses, and making it very much worse to walk than in a saw-pit newly used. However, we trudged along in a line; I first, and the other men after me; trying to keep my track, but finding legs and strength not up to it. Most of all, John Fry was groaning; certain that his time was come, and sending messages to his wife, and blessings to his children. For all this time it was snowing harder than it had ever snowed before, so far as a man might guess at it; and the leaden depth of sky came down, like a mine turned upside down on us. Not that the flakes were so very large; for I have seen much larger flakes in a shower in March, while sowing peas; but there was no room between them, neither any relaxing, nor any change of direction.

Watch, like a good and faithful dog, followed us very cheerfully, leaping out of the depth which took him over his back and ears already, even in the level places; while in the

17

# · A West Country Christmas ·

Exmoor in the grip of winter

drifts he might have sunk to any distance out of sight and never found his way up again. However, we helped him now and then, especially through the gaps and gateways; and so after a deal of floundering, some laughter and a little swearing, we came safe to the lower meadow, where most of our flock were hurdled.

But behold, there was no flock at all! None, I mean, to be seen anywhere; only at one corner of the field, by the eastern end, where the snow drove in, a great white billow, as high as a barn and as broad as a house. This great drift was rolling and curling beneath the violent blast, tufting and coming with rustling swirls, and carved (as in patterns of cornice) where the grooving chisel of the wind swept round. Ever and again, the tempest snatched little whiffs from the channelled edges, twirled them round, and made them dance over the chine of the monster pile, then let them lie like herring-bones, or the seams of sand where the tide had been. And all the while from the smothering sky, more and more fiercely at every blast, came the pelting pitiless arrows, winged with murky white, and pointed with barbs of frost.

But although, for people who had no sheep, the sight was a very fine one (so far at least as the weather permitted any sight at all); yet for us, with our flock beneath it, this great mount had but little charm. Watch began to scratch at once, and to howl along the sides of it; he knew that his charge was buried there, and his business taken from him. But we four men set to in earnest, digging with all our might and main, shovelling away at the great white pile, and fetching it into the meadow. Each man made for himself a cave, scooping at the soft cold flux, which slid upon him at every stroke, and throwing it out behind him, in piles of castled fancy. At last we drove our tunnels in (for we worked indeed for the lives of us), and all converging towards the middle, held our tools and listened.

The other men heard nothing at all; or declared that they heard nothing, being anxious now to abandon the matter, because of the chill in their feet and knees. But I said, 'Go, if you choose, all of you. I will work it out by myself, you pie-crusts': and upon that they gripped their shovels, being more or less Englishmen; and the least drop of English blood is worth the best of any other, when it comes to lasting out.

But before we began again, I laid my head well into the chamber; and there I heard a faint 'ma-a-ah', coming through some ells of snow, like a plaintive buried hope, or a last appeal. I shouted aloud to cheer him up, for I knew what sheep it was, to wit the most valiant of all the wethers, who had met me when I came home from London, and had been so glad to see me. And then we all fell to again; and very soon we hauled him out. Watch took charge of him at once, with an air of noblest patronage, lying on his frozen fleece, and licking him

*19*

*Sixty-and-six I took home in that way, two at a time.*

The rescue of the sheep, drawn by Lionel Edwards; from
'The Great Winter', *Lorna Doone*, chapter XLII

all over his face and feet, to restore his warmth to him. Then
fighting Tom jumped up at once, and made a little butt at
Watch, as if nothing had ever ailed him, and then set off to a
shallow place, and looked for something to nibble at.

Further in, and close under the bank, where they had
huddled themselves for warmth, we found all the rest of the
poor sheep packed as closely as if they were in a great pie. It
was strange to observe how their vapour, and breath, the
moisture exuding from their wool, had scooped, as it were, a
covered room for them, lined with a ribbing of deep yellow
snow. Also the churned snow beneath their feet was as yellow
as gamboge. Two or three of the weaklier hoggets were dead,
from want of air, and from pressure; but more than three score
were as lively as ever: though cramped and stiff for a little
while.

'However shall we get them home?' John Fry asked in great dismay, when we had cleared about a dozen of them; which we were forced to do very carefully, so as not to fetch the roof down. 'No manner of manning to draive 'un, drough all they giry driftnesses.'

'You see to this place, John,' I replied, as we leaned on our shovels a moment, and the sheep came rubbing around us: 'Let no more of them out for the present; they are better where they be. Watch, here boy, keep them!'

Watch came, and with his little scut of a tail cocked as sharp a duty; and I set him at the narrow mouth of the great snow antre. All the sheep siddled away, and got closer, that the other sheep might be bitten first, as the foolish things imagine; whereas no good sheep-dog even so much as lips a sheep to turn it.

Then of the outer sheep (all now snowed and frizzled like a lawyer's wig) I took the two finest and heaviest; and with one beneath my right arm, and the other beneath my left, I went straight home to the upper sheppey, set them inside and fastened them. Sixty-and-six I took home in that way, two at a time on each journey; and the work grew harder and harder each time, as the drifts of snow were deepening. No man should meddle with them: I was resolved to try my strength against the strength of the elements; and try I did, ay and proved it. A certain fierce delight burned in me, as the struggle grew harder; but rather would I die than yield; and at last I finished it. People talk of it to this day; but none can tell what the labour was, who had not felt that snow and wind.

The cliffs at Hillsborough on the North Devon coast,
Winter 1940

# The Holly and the Ivy

*'The Holly and the Ivy' is a traditional carol which has
probably been around for centuries in one form or another.
It was re-discovered and recorded by Cecil Sharp, an
archivist of folklore and country songs — he collected over
5,000 — when he copied down the words and music from a
Mrs Clayton of Chipping Campden in Gloucestershire.
Extra words were added by a Mrs Wyatt of East Harptree
in Somerset, so the carol can truly be said to have its origins
in the West Country.*

# · A West Country Christmas ·

The Holly and the Ivy
When they are both full grown
Of all the trees that are in the wood,
The Holly bears a crown:

*The rising of the sun*
*And the running of the deer*
*The playing of the merry organ*
*Sweet singing in the choir.*

The Holly bears a blossom
As white as the lily flower
And Mary bore sweet Jesus Christ
To be our sweet saviour:

The Holly bears a berry
As red as any blood
And Mary bore sweet Jesus Christ,
To do poor sinners good:

The Holly bears a prickle
As sharp as any thorn
And Mary bore sweet Jesus Christ
On Christmas Day in the morn:

The Holly bears a bark
As bitter as any gall,
And Mary bore sweet Jesus Christ
For to redeem us all:

The Holly and the Ivy
When they are both full grown
Of all the trees that are in the wood,
The Holly bears a crown.

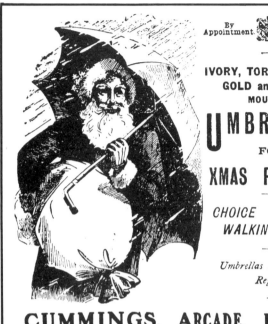
# Christmas for the Choir

*With our ears still ringing from that wonderful carol, let's just spare a thought for those who have to work, even on Christmas Day. One Christmas, a few years ago, I*

*saw a television programme which featured people whose jobs meant that they couldn't relax and enjoy Christmas as so many of us are able to do. Those who had to carry on working included farmers, doctors, nurses, police and firemen. In fact, the list seemed endless, and the programme alerted me to the number of people who have to celebrate Christmas while carrying on with their everyday work. Doubtless somewhere along the way, during the course of the day, they managed to snatch a short time in which to mark the occasion, but work came first.*

*Amongst those for whom Christmas is not exactly a rest period are choirboys. In fact, they probably work harder at Christmas than at any other time in the church's year. The 'Schola Cantorum', as the old Choristers' School in Exeter was called in the thirteenth century, has been situated near the Cathedral Close in the city for some 700 years. Originally the school's sole purpose was the education of choirboys, but in the 1950s it was decided to admit non-choristers as well, and today Exeter Cathedral School caters for more than 160 boys aged between seven and thirteen, including twenty-five choristers, with a quarter of the pupils being boarders.*

*Obviously Christmas is a big event in the life of an Exeter Cathedral School chorister, and here two of the senior choirboys, Tim Soper and Andrew Dobbins, both aged thirteen, recall the 'run up' to last Christmas.*

*December 20th.* Now only five days until Christmas and we're already getting tired and we haven't really started yet.
8.30 to 9.45 a.m. Another choir practice for us to attend – luckily, it's during our Latin lesson!
9.55 a.m. It's back to boring old lessons again and once more we have to start the day with French. Anyway, so what? It's the last day of term today.

3.45 p.m. After an end of term service in the Cathedral, school breaks up. We choristers have to watch all our friends go home. We've got to stay until Boxing Day, which at the moment seems a long way off.

5.30 p.m. Evensong in the Cathedral as usual which is followed by supper.

7.00 p.m. After supper we all go to a performance of the Christmas play at the local theatre – The Northcott. It's a lot more relaxing than practice, a service or lessons.

10.00 p.m. Arrive back at the boarding house. Everybody is shattered. It's been a long day!

*December 21st.* It's getting nearer. We're feeling a bit sad because everybody except us choristers is at home now with their families. You can't help wondering what they're doing and thinking that they're having a good time while we've got to work. But one good thing is that today we're going to be allowed out with our parents for a whole day, but first:

8.45 a.m. Breakfast, which takes half an hour and is followed by a full scale practice in the Cathedral of an hour and a quarter. A day out and freedom. Time to forget about singing and enjoy ourselves.

8.30 p.m. Back to the boarding house. It's been a good but exhausting day. Say good-bye to our parents before turning in for another night's rest. Tomorrow's another day.

*December 22nd.* Breakfast as usual, which is followed at 9.30 a.m. by another long practice in the Cathedral for the Grandisson Service on Christmas Eve.

11.00 a.m. Leave for an outing to Torquay. The Leisure Centre is the first stop. We can play badminton, squash and five-a-side football. There's swimming as well. Who said

choirboys aren't fit? After that it's off to the skateboard park just up the road from the Leisure Centre.

4.30 p.m. Back to the Cathedral for another practice. It's for Evensong.

5.30 p.m. Evensong, which is followed by supper. All that activity and then the service has made everybody very hungry. After supper the rest of the evening is free until bedtime. A chance to unwind and relax a bit.

*December 23rd.* Guess what? We start the day with breakfast.

9.30 to 10.45 a.m. Another full practice for the choir for Christmas Day Carols.

11.00 a.m. We were supposed to go shopping but the shopping trip was postponed. Shame, we were looking forward to that. Instead we go to another Leisure Centre, Barnstaple this time. More activity.

3.30 p.m. Rest (we need it after the trip to the Leisure Centre and all that swimming) for the big practice after Evensong.

5.30 p.m. Evensong as usual. Today with a difference though as Mr Nethsingha, our choirmaster, walked out. Some of us thought it was because our singing was so bad that he simply couldn't take any more!

6.20 p.m. It's going to be another late night again. Mr Nethsingha has decided to have an extra practice which finishes around 7.30 p.m.

7.45 p.m. Supper – Bangers and mash. You can't beat that can you? Wonder if we'll have sausages with our turkey on Christmas Day?

*December 24th. Christmas Eve.* As usual we start the day with breakfast and then guess what? Another practice.

9.30 to 10.45 a.m. This is a practice for the special Grand-isson Service. It's very tiring and it will be one of the most

Exeter Cathedral Choir

important services of the year, when the Cathedral will be packed with people to listen to the carols and the reading of the lessons.

11.00 a.m. Free time! A last chance to buy presents, cards or even sweets!

1.00 p.m. After lunch we go off on an outing – to nearby woods this time.

3.30 p.m. When we get back we are supposed to have a rest – Boring! Then tea. Then it's time to get ready for the Grandisson Service. We all have showers, there's clean clothes to put on, we've got to polish our shoes extra hard till they shine like our clean hair which we have to comb and brush and for those with colds or a sore throat there's a dose of medicine (if you like it).

6.00 p.m. At last – it's here. The Grandisson Service. It seems we've been preparing for this for ages and now it's come. The Service actually lasts for about one and a half hours, but it seems to get progressively shorter every time.

7.30 p.m. After the Service it's back to the boarding houses, with our parents and close family who have come to the Cathedral, for some refreshments and mince pies. It now really feels as if Christmas is here. Then there is a bit of entertainment. Every boy and parent is given the theme of one of the twelve days of Christmas which usually gives everybody a laugh. And we're allowed to open one present, because some parents live too far way to visit even on Christmas Day. It's a jolly family atmosphere to end the day. It's been tiring but fun and then it's bed and lights out and try to get some sleep. Tomorrow is of course Christmas Day.

*December 25th. Christmas Day.* 5.30 a.m. Father Christmas has been and it's time to open our presents!!! After an early start it's breakfast at 8.30 a.m.

9.00 a.m. Return to the boarding houses for the boys to put the copies out in the Cathedral for Eucharist at 9.45 a.m. and for Matins at 11.00 a.m.

9.45 a.m. Eucharist. Not a bad Eucharist either, we had to sing Schubert's Mass in G. An extra long Eucharist because of so many people. It means missing out on our orange and biscuits.

11.15 a.m. Early morning Matins for an hour.

12.30 p.m. The highlight of the day? Christmas lunch. Heaped plates of turkey and stuffing and all the trimmings.

3.25 p.m. Boys return to the Cathedral to put out the copies for Evensong.

4.00 p.m. Evensong along with carols sung from the Minstrels' gallery. Evensong lasts about an hour and a quarter and then we return to the boarding houses again to see our parents, if they've managed to make the trip. Free time until a big meal in the evening with lots of guests and visitors.

9.00 p.m. Straight to bed. It's home tomorrow.


*December 26th. Boxing Day.* 8.00 a.m. Last breakfast of the term followed by 8.45 a.m. Last practice of the term for the last service.

9.30 a.m. Sung Eucharist at which parents are invited to take Holy Communion with their sons.

10.30 a.m. At last. It's time for us to leave for our Christmas holiday. That's of course if parents haven't forgotten about you or the car hasn't broken down! It's been hard work and good fun – but then that's Christmas.

*from*

# Under the Greenwood Tree

## THOMAS HARDY

*Thomas Hardy, a son of Dorset and Dorchester immortalized the West Country of his day through the Wessex of his novels, stories and poems, His* Under the Greenwood Tree, *published in 1872, is subtitled* The Mellstock Quire. *It is the story of a group of church musicians — both instrumentalists and singers — who, in return for little payment, whatever the weather, make their way on foot from far and wide to the church every Sunday. A true labour of love, for, as Thomas Hardy wrote, 'In the parish that I had in mind when writing the present tale the gratuities received yearly by the musicians at Christmas were somewhat as follows: From the manor-house, ten shillings and a supper; from the vicar, ten shillings; from each cottage-household one shilling; amounting altogether to not more than ten shillings a head annually — just enough, as an old executant told me, to pay for their fiddle-strings, repairs, rosin and music-paper (which they mostly ruled themselves). Their music in those days was all in their own manuscript, copied in the*

# · A West Country Christmas ·

*evenings after work, and their music-books were home bound.' In this chapter from* Under the Greenwood Tree, *the Mellstock Quire are 'Going the Rounds'.*

Shortly after ten o'clock the singing-boys arrived at the tranter's house, which was invariably the place of meeting, and preparations were made for the start. The older men and musicians wore thick coats, with stiff perpendicular collars, and coloured handkerchiefs wound round and round the neck till the end came to hand, over all which they just showed their ears and noses, like people looking over a wall. The remainder, stalwart ruddy men and boys, were dressed mainly in snow-white smock-frocks, embroidered upon the shoulders and breasts in ornamental forms of hearts, diamonds, and zigzags. The cider-mug was emptied for the ninth time, the music-books were arranged and the pieces finally decided upon. The boys in the meantime put the old horn-lanterns in order, cut the candles into short lengths to fit the lanterns; and, a thin fleece of snow having fallen since the early part of the evening, those who had no leggings went to the stable and wound wisps of hay round their ankles to keep the insidious flakes from the interior of their boots.

Mellstock was a parish of considerable acreage, the hamlets composing it laying at a much greater distance from each other than is ordinarily the case. Hence several hours were consumed in playing and singing within the hearing of every family, even if but a single air were bestowed on each. There was Lower Mellstock, the main village; half a mile from this were the church and vicarage, and a few other houses, the spot being rather lonely now, though in past centuries it had been the most thickly-populated quarter of the parish. A mile north-east lay the hamlet of Upper Mellstock, where the tranter lived; and at other points knots of cottages, besides solitary farmsteads and dairies.

Old William Dewy, with the violoncello, played the bass; his grandson Dick the treble violin; and Ruben and Michael Mail the tenor and second violins respectively. The singers consisted of four men and seven boys, upon whom devolved the task of carrying and attending to the lanterns, and holding the books open for the players. Directly music was the theme, old William ever and instinctively came to the front.

'Now mind, neighbours,' he said, as they all went out one by one at the door, he himself holding it ajar and regarding them with a critical face as they passed, like a shepherd counting out his sheep. 'You two counter-boys, keep your ears open to Michael's fingering, and don't ye go straying into the treble part along o'Dick and his set, as ye did last year; and mind this especially when we be in "Arise, and hail." Billy Chimlen, don't you sing quite so raving mad as you fain would; and, all o'ye, whatever ye do, keep from making a great scuffle on the ground when we go in at people's gates; but go quietly, so as to strike up all of a sudden, like spirits.'

'Farmer Ludlow's first?'

'Farmer Ludlow's first; the rest as usual.'

'And, Voss,' said the tranter terminatively, 'you keep house here till about half-past two; then heat the metheglin and cider in the warmer you'll find turned up upon the copper; and bring it wi' the victuals to church hatch, as th'st know.'

Just before the clock struck twelve they lighted the lanterns and started. The moon, in her third quarter, had risen since the snowstorm; but the dense accumulation of snow-cloud weakened her power to a faint twilight, which was rather pervasive of the landscape than traceable to the sky. The breeze had gone down, and the rustle of their feet and tones of their speech echoed with an alert rebound from every post, boundary-stone, and ancient wall they passed, even where the distance of the echo's origin was less than a few yards. Beyond their own slight noises nothing was to be heard, save the

# · *A West Country Christmas* ·

As the Mellstock Quire must have looked 'Going the Rounds'

occasional bark of the foxes in the direction of Yalbury Wood, or the brush of a rabbit among the grass now and then, as it scampered out of their way.

Most of the outlying homesteads and hamlets had been visited by two o'clock; they then passed across the outskirts of a wooded park toward the main village, nobody being at home at the Manor. Pursuing no recognized track, great care was necessary in walking lest their faces should come into contact with the low-hanging boughs of the old lime-trees, which in many spots formed dense overgrowths of interlaced branches.

'Times have changed from the times they used to be,' said Mail, regarding nobody can tell what interesting panoramas with an inward eye, and letting his outward glance rest on the ground, because it was as convenient a position as any. 'People don't care much about us now! I've been thinking we must be almost the last left in the country of the old string players? Barrel-organs, and the things next door to 'em that you blow wi' your foot, have come in terribly of late years.'

'Ay!' said Bowman, shaking his head; and old William, on seeing him, did the same thing.

'More's the pity,' replied another. 'Time was – long and merry ago now! – when not one of the varmits was to be heard of; but it served some of the quires right. They should have stuck to strings as we did, and kept out clarinets, and done away with serpents. If you'd thrive in musical religion, stick to strings, says I.'

'Strings be safe soul-lifters, as far as that do go,' said Mr Spinks.

'Yet there's worse things than serpents,' said Mr Penny. 'Old things pass away, 'tis true; but a serpent was a good old note: a deep rich note was the serpent.'

'Clar'nets, however, be bad at all times,' said Michael Mail. 'One Christmas – years agone now, years – I went the rounds wi' the Weatherbury quire. 'Twas a hard frosty night, and the keys of all the clar'nets froze – ah, they did freeze! – so that 'twas like drawing a cork every time a key was opened; and the players o' 'em had to go into a hedger-and-ditcher's chimley-corner, and thaw their clar'nets every now and then. An icicle o'spet hung down from the end of every man's clar'net a span long; and as to fingers – well, there, if ye'll believe me, we had no fingers at all, to our knowing.'

'I can well bring back to my mind,' said Mr Penny, 'what I

said to poor Joseph Ryme (who took the treble part in Chalk-Newton Church for two-and-forty year) when they thought of having clar'nets there. "Joseph," I said, says I, "depend upon't, if so be you have them tooting clar'nets you'll spoil the whole set-out. Clar'nets were not made for the service of the Lard; you can see by looking at 'em," I said. And what came o't ? Why, souls, the parson set up a barrel-organ on his own account within two years o' the time I spoke, and the old quire went to nothing.'

'As far as look is concerned,' said the tranter, 'I don't for my part see that a fiddle is much nearer heaven than a clar'net. 'Tis further off. There's always a rakish, scampish twist about a fiddle's looks that seems to say the Wicked One had a hand in making o'en; while angels be supposed to play clar'nets in heaven, or som'at like 'em, if ye may believe the picters.'

'Robert Penny, you was in the right,' broke in the eldest Dewy. 'They should ha' stuck to strings. Your bass-man is a rafting dog – well and good; your reed-man is a dab at stirring ye – well and good; your drum-man is a rare bowel-shaker – good again. But I don't care who hears me say it, nothing will spak to your heart wi' the sweetness o' the man of strings!'

'Strings for ever!' said little Jimmy.

'Strings alone would have held their ground against all new comers in creation.' ('True, true!' said Bowman.) 'But clarinets was death.' ('Death they was!' said Mr Penny.) 'And harmonions,' William continued in a louder voice, and getting excited by these signs of approval, 'harmonions and barrel-organs' ('Ah!' and groans from Spinks) 'be miserable – what shall I call 'em? – miserable —'

'Sinners,' suggested Jimmy, who made large strides like the men, and did not lag behind like the other little boys.

'Miserable dumbledores!'

'Right, William, and so they be – miserable dumbledores!' said the choir with unanimity.

Thomas Hardy's cottage at Higher Bockhampton, Dorset

By this time they were crossing to a gate in the direction of the school, which, standing on a slight eminence at the junction of three ways, now rose in unvarying and dark flatness against the sky. The instruments were returned, and all the band entered the school enclosure, enjoined by old William to keep upon the grass.

'Number seventy-eight,' he softly gave out as they formed round in a semicircle, the boys opening the lanterns to get a clearer light, and directing their rays on the books.

They passed forth into the quiet night an ancient and time-worn hymn, embodying a quaint Christianity in words orally transmitted from father to son through several generations down to the present characters, who sang them out right earnestly:

# · A West Country Christmas ·

Remember Adam's fall
O thou Man:
Remember Adam's fall
From Heaven to Hell.
Remember Adam's fall;
How he hath condemn'd all
In Hell perpetual
There for to dwell.

Remember God's goodnesse,
O thou Man:
Remember God's goodnesse,
His promise made.
Remember God's goodnesse;
He sent His Son sinlesse,
Our ails for to redress;
Be not afraid!

In Bethlehem He was born,
O thou Man:
In Bethlehem He was born,
For mankind's sake.
In Bethlehem He was born
Christmas-day i' the morn:
Our Saviour thought no scorn
Our faults to take.

Give thanks to God alway
O thou Man:
Give thanks to God alway
With heart-most joy.
Give thanks to God alway
On this our Joyful Day:
Let all men sing and say,
Holy, Holy!

# The Tradition of Wassailing

Cider has long been a part of life in the West Country where at one time most farms used to boast their own cider-apple orchard. At the turn of the year, Christmas Eve or New Year's Eve, the custom of wassailing took place. The word 'wassail' is derived from the Anglo-Saxon 'waes hale', meaning 'be whole' or 'be of good health'. Today we shorten it to 'good health' or 'cheers'.

Wassailing was a ceremony which was believed to ensure a good crop of apples for the coming season. It consisted of offerings being made to the spirits of the apple trees. The offerings were always accompanied by wassailing verses or songs.

> Here's to thee, old apple-tree
> Whence thou may'st bud.
> And whence thou may'st blow!
> And whence thou may'st bear apples enow!
> Hats full! Caps full!
> Bushel-bushel-sacks full!
> And my pockets full too! Hooray!

In addition to the offerings and singing, a great deal of noise

was made by banging and beating pots and pans to frighten away the evil spirits, and guns were even fired into the branches of the apple trees.

> Old Apple tree
> We wassail thee and hoping thou will bear,
> For the Lord doth know where we shall be
> Till apples come another year,
> For to bear well and to bloom well,
> So merry let us be,
> Let every man take off his hat
> And shout out to the old apple tree.

The offerings would be of toast soaked in cider which were then placed in the branches of the tree which it was thought would encourage the good spirits in the form of the robin – a traditional symbol of Christmas – and then cider, often mulled or heated, would be splashed around the roots of the tree and the ceremony would be repeated round all the trees in the orchard. Sometimes the trees would be pelted with rotten apples and even threats made to destroy the tree if it did not bear well.

> Apple tree, apple tree,
> Bear good fruit,
> Or down with your top,
> And up with your root.

The ceremony seems to have remained unchanged and with little variation throughout the West Country, although it is recorded that in some parts a small boy would be hoisted up into the branches where he recited: 'Tit, tit, more to eat.'

The Taunton Cider Company, based at Norton Fitzwarren in Somerset, revived the custom of wassailing which has all

but died out in the West Country – perhaps not unconnected with the virtual disappearance of the farm cider orchards – some seventeen years ago, and the photograph shows the Wassail Queen of 1989, Cherie Wildman, perched on the shoulders of her escorts, dipping the toast into the mulled cider before placing it in the branches of the tree.

After Christmas, another West Country tradition is that of Visiting Wassails – a group getting together and visiting houses in the neighbourhood where they could be certain of a warm welcome, a sort of forerunner to the modern day carol singers. They would sing wassailing songs and drink the health of the householder before moving on, probably ending up in the village inn or pub. Not a lot changes, does it?

Cherie Wildman, Taunton Cider Company's Wassail Queen of 1989

# · *A West Country Christmas* ·

Now Christmas is over, our Wassail begin.
Pray, open your door and let us come in.

Now we poor wassail boys are growing weary and cold
Drop a small piece of silver into our bowl.

I hope that your apple trees will prosper and bear,
And bring forth good cider when we come next year.

Wassail, oh wassail all over the town
The cup it is white and the ale it is brown
The cup it is made of the good old ashen tree
And so is the beer of the best barley.

For its your wassail
And its our, our wassail
And I'm jolly come to our jolly wassail.

God bless Missus and Master and all the family.
Wishing you a happy Christmas
And a bright and prosperous New Year.

For those who would like to revive further the tradition of
wassailing, but need some encouragement in the form of
liquid refreshment, here's a recipe for **A Wassail Cup**. You'll
need:

6 pints of cider or ale
1 lb of brown sugar
1 large stick of cinnamon
Grated nutmeg – to taste
½ level teaspoon of ground ginger (to add the bite)
2 lemons thinly sliced
1 bottle of sherry – dry/medium according to taste

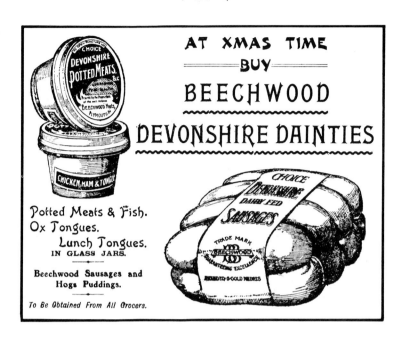

Pour half the cider into a large saucepan and heat, adding the brown sugar and the stick of cinnamon. Simmer the mixture until the sugar has dissolved and then add the rest of the cider and the sherry, together with the other spices. Finally add the lemon slices and float roasted apples in the pan before serving with a ladle. That's your **Wassail Cup**.

If your wassail is successful and your apple trees bear well, here is **Madam's Receipt to make Cyder**, taken from a handwritten book dated 1803:

First pound your apples early in the morning and lay them up immediately. When the cyder comes from the cheese, put it directly into a large vessel to ferment and let it remain until it works up white and comes clear under. Then, drain

it off and throw it into hogsheads.

Let it remain in the hogsheads until it is perfectly fine again. This must be done three times to prevent the fermentation. Secondly choice of apples – let the apples remain until they begin to rot but those that are entirely rotten must be thrown away.

On the other hand, you may prefer to buy it in a bottle! Whichever, I hope that this Christmas you will most certainly be 'waes hale' and 'of good health'. Cheers!

# Christmas 1862

## SABINE BARING-GOULD

*It would seem that no Visiting Wassails or carol singers
called on the manor-house at Lew Trenchard in Devon in
1862 to brighten the Christmas of Sabine Baring-Gould
who was staying in the parish, where his father was rector
and of which he was to become rector in 1881. In fact his
diary records a fairly bleak occasion, without any sign of
a wassail cup to warm the heart.*

Christmas Day alone except for my little brother in Lew House. The rats were celebrating *Noël*. They had a frolic last night, kept high festival, had a wild hunt. They scoured along the passages, they scampered between floor and ceiling, they

danced a hornpipe in the storeroom and rollicked up and down the stairs. They kept me awake. Presently I heard the distant strains of carol-singers and the groaning of an accompanying bass-viol. I ascertained in the morning that the performers were the choir of the meeting house. The church, buried in sleep, did not sing to greet the Saviour's birth. The chapel choir itinerated all night till 5 o'clock in the morning. They visited every house in the parish except those of the Parson and the Squire, for the former was too orthodox to tolerate dissenting music and the latter was absent from home. At their return they were all the worse for liquor. In church this morning there were twelve persons, of these nearly all were from the rectory.

The Revd and Mrs Puckeridge of Pinhoe, also in Devon, were a bit more cheerful than Sabine Baring-Gould, in spite of the war, as this Christmas card of 1942, with personal photograph and greeting shows

# Christmas Day

## CHARLES KINGSLEY

*The weather is often something that is in people's minds at Christmas time. Will it snow? Will we have a white Christmas? The following poem by Charles Kingsley (and there is more from his pen later) shows that little has changed over the years.*

How will it dawn, the coming Christmas Day?
A Northern Christmas, such as painters love,
And kinsmen, shaking hands but once a year,
And dames who tell old legends by the fire?
Red sun, blue sky, white snow, and pearled ice,
Keen ringing air, which sets the blood on fire,
And makes the old man merry with the young,
Through the short sunshine, through the longer night?

Or Southern Christmas, dark and dank with mist,
And heavy with the scent of steaming leaves,
And rose buds mouldering on the dripping porch;
One twilight, without the rise or set of sun,
Till beetles drone along the hollow lane,
And round the leafless hawthorns, flitting bats
Hawk the pale moths of winter? Welcome then
At best, the flying gleam, the flying shower,
The rain-pools glittering on the long white roads,

And shadows sweeping on from down to down
Before the salt Atlantic gale: yet to come
In whatsoever garb, or gay, or sad,
Come fair or foul, 'twill still be Christmas Day.

# Weather Wisdom

Aside from wondering what weather Christmas itself would bring, there were those in the West Country who thought that the weather on Christmas Day foretold the weather of the future. In *Weather Wisdom*, published in 1889, we are told, 'A green Christmas, a white Easter', and, 'A Saturday's Christmas is supposed to bring about a foggy winter and a cold summer.' According to a volume of the Devon Association of 1880:

> Hours of sunshine on Christmas Day,
> So many frosts in the month of May.

Weather forecasting, it was said, could also be based on the day of the week on which Christmas fell, as Gervase Markham wrote in his *Second Booke of English Husbandman* of 1614: 'If Christmas fall upon a Thursday, the year shall be temperate and healthy but the summer shall be rainy.' Over two centuries later, in 1863, W.I.S. Horton wrote:

> If Christmas Day on Thursday be
> A windy winter we shall see;

# · *A West Country Christmas* ·

Windy weather in each week
And hard tempests strong and thick;
The summer shall be good and dry,
Corn and beasts shall multiply.

However:

If Christmas Day on Monday be
A great winter that year you'll see,
Full of winds both loud and shrill;
But in summer truth to tell,
High winds there shall be and strong,
Full of tempests lasting long;
While battles they shall multiply,
And great plenty of beasts shall die.
They that be born that day, I wean
They shall be strong each one and keen
He shall be found that stealeth aught;
Though thou be sick, thou diest not.

# Winter Weather

## WILLIAM BARNES

*William Barnes was born into a farming family near Sturminster Newton, Dorset, in 1801. Having left school, he worked as a solicitor's clerk before becoming a schoolmaster, and with his wife Julia he ran a very successful school in Dorchester. In 1844, he published a collection of rural poems in Dorset dialect which brought him national recognition and earned him the admiration of Thomas Hardy himself. In 1862, he became rector of Winterbourne Came and remained there until his death in 1886. The following poem, although not in dialect, perfectly evokes Christmas and the winter coming to the Dorset countryside over one hundred years ago.*

When stems of elms may rise in row
Dark brown, from hillocks under snow,
And woods may reach as black as night
By sloping fields of clearest white.
If shooters by the snowy rick,
Where trees are high, and wood is thick,
Can mark the tracks the game may pick,
They like the winter weather.

Or where may spread the grey-blue sheet
Of ice, for skaters' gliding feet,
That they uplift, from side to side

Long yards, and hit them down to slide
Or sliders, one that totters slack
Of limb, and one that's on his back.
And one that upright keeps his track,
Have fun in winter weather.

When we at night, in snow and gloom,
May see some neighbour's lighted room.
Though snow may show no path before
The house, we still can find the door,
And there, as round the brands may spread
The creeping fire of cherry red,
Our feet from snow, from wind our head
Are warm in winter weather.

Whatever day may give our road,
By hills and hollows oversnow'd
By windy gaps, or sheltered nooks,
Or bridged ice of frozen brooks,
Still may we all, as night may come
Know where to find a peaceful home,
And glowing fire for fingers numb
With cold in winter weather.

*from*

# Westward Ho!

## CHARLES KINGSLEY

*It's no surprise to find that the tiny North Devon seaside village of Clovelly features in so many West Country pictorial calendars. Clovelly, with its narrow, cobbled main street, is almost breath-taking in its beauty. In the winter, the village is quiet, totally unspoilt, and free of both tourists and traffic. This is the season to visit and to step back in time, to smell the wood-smoke in the air and wonder how twentieth-century life has passed this place by. Life here really hasn't changed a great deal over the years — true, the herring, which used to be the chief trade of the fishing boats which still work out of the harbour nestling below the village, have largely disappeared — but it would be hard to imagine a place better suited to spending a Christmas away from it all, shut safe and cosy behind one of the cottage doors in front of a crackling log fire, in good company, and with food and wine to match. Outside, though, the chances are that the elements will not be so settled. The weather here can be fierce, with howling winds and driving rain coming in from the sea and lashing the picturesque houses and walled harbour, but at Christmas time, with any luck, the gales are still to come, and Clovelly rests at peace.*

# · *A West Country Christmas* ·

Clovelly in the snow

*In 1831 Charles Kingsley the elder came to Clovelly as a curate, and it was one of his three sons, also Charles by name, who was perhaps most responsible for putting Clovelly 'on the map' through his book* Westward Ho! *In this extract he paints a vivid picture of the peace and well-being of Christmas Day with the storms of winter about to break. In his book, as in Clovelly, the sea is never far away . . .*

## How Amyas kept his Christmas Day

It was the blessed Christmas afternoon. The light was fading down; the even-song was done; and the good folks of Bideford were trooping home in merry groups, the father with his children, the lover with his sweetheart, to cakes and ales, and flapdragons and mummer's plays, and all the happy sports of Christmas night. One lady only, wrapped close in her black muffler, and followed by her maid, walked swiftly, yet sadly, toward the long causeway and bridge which led to Northam town. Sir Richard Grenville and his wife caught her up and stopped her courteously.

'You will come home with us, Mrs Leigh,' said Lady Grenville, 'and spend a pleasant Christmas night?'

Mrs Leigh smiled sweetly, and laying one hand on Mrs Grenville's arm, pointed with the other to the westward, and said, —

'I cannot well spend a merry Christmas night while that sound is in my ears.'

The whole party looked around in the direction in which she pointed. Above their heads the soft blue sky was fading into grey, and here and there a misty star peeped out; but to the westward, where the downs and woods of Raleigh closed with those of Abbotsham, the blue was webbed and tufted with delicate white flakes; iridescent spots, marking the path by which the sun had sunk, showed all the colours of the dying dolphin; and low on the horizon lay a long band of grassy green.

But what was the sound that troubled Mrs Leigh? None of them, with their merry hearts, and ears dulled with the din and bustle of the town, had heard it till that moment; and yet now – listen! It was dead calm. There was not a breath to stir a blade of grass. And yet the air was full of sound – a low, deep roar which hovered over down and wood, salt marsh and river, like a roll of a thousand wheels, the tramp of endless armies, or – what it was – the thunder of a mighty surge upon the boulders of the pebble ridge.

'The ridge is noisy to-night,' said Sir Richard. 'There has been wind somewhere.'

'There is wind now, where my boy is, God help him!' said

# · A West Country Christmas ·

Clovelly street, 1802

54

Mrs Leigh; and all knew that she spoke truly. The spirit of the Atlantic storm had sent forward the token of his coming, in the smooth ground-swell which was heard inland, two miles away. Tomorrow the pebbles, which were now rattling down with each retreating wave, might be leaping up to the ridge top, and hurled like round-shot far ashore upon the marsh by the force of the advancing wave, fleeing before the wrath of the western hurricane.

'God help my boy!' said Mrs Leigh again.

'God is as near him by sea as by land,' said good Sir Richard.

'True, but I am a lone mother, and one that has no heart just now but to go home and pray.'

And so Mrs Leigh went onward up the lane, and spent all that night in listening between her prayers to the thunder of the surge, till it was drowned, long ere the sun rose, in the thunder of the storm.

And where is Amyas on this same Christmas afternoon?

Amyas is sitting bareheaded in a boat's stern in Smerwick Bay, with the spray whistling through his curls, as he shouts cheerfully, —

'Pull, and with a will, my merry men all, and never mind shipping a sea. Canon balls are a cargo that don't spoil by taking salt water.'

His mother's presage had been true enough. Christmas Eve had been the last of the still, dark, steaming nights of early winter; and the western gale has been roaring for the last twelve hours upon the Irish coast.

*from*

# Christmas in Cornwall Sixty Years Ago

## MRS JOHN BONHAM

*From the North Devon coast we go now to Cornwall, where the seas can be equally inhospitable, and to a tale which was published in 1898 and was unearthed for me by a librarian who drew it to my attention. I'm grateful, for this slim volume by the author of* A Corner of Old Cornwall *is a little gem.*

### Christmas Eve

The Christmas Eve that stands out before all others, and is even now referred to with emotion by the very oldest inhabitant of St Cadge, was that on which a great sorrow fell on the entire neighbourhood.

It was between two and three in the afternoon, and there was an ugly ground swell in the Cove.

Two crabbers – brothers, who had gone to Rackover to fetch a boatload of withes for making their crabpots – now made for the Cove in their heavily-laden boat. They were men much respected, especially the elder brother, who was a sincere Christian and whose consistent life and kindly disposition had endeared him to his neighbours.

There were many speculations among those on shore as to the risk of landing with such a sea, but none seemed to think it necessary to warn them by signs not to approach. On came the boat, and cautiously the two men watched their opportunity to run her in between one wave and another.

The beach was filled with anxious watchers, among them the son and two daughters of the elder brother; all of them excited, but not realising the awful risk to which the two men were exposed. After keeping the boat tolerably stationary for some minutes, and then taking advantage of a temporary lull, they exerted all their strength and pulled vigorously for the shore.

Alas! The task was too great. A hugh wave behind curled over, entirely swamping the boat. Everybody stood panic-stricken and riveted to the spot. Then the three children rushed wildly up and down; Mattie, her father's pet, falling heavily into some woman's arms. Both men were seen to rise, striking vigorously at first with their hands; but neither of them could swim. Presently the hands moved more feebly, and then altogether disappeared.

Meanwhile a young and courageous fisherman had hurriedly launched a boat, which was put off, and the bodies were quickly picked up.

All that could possibly be done to restore life was resorted to, but the improved methods of inducing respiration, little enough understood by a crowd even in our own day, were then scarcely known or practised at all, and the unfortunate men finally succumbed.

Mattie recovered consciousness just as they were engaged in rescuing the drowning men. As soon as they were brought ashore, she sank down by the body of her father, fixing her eyes intently on his face, and watching for the least sign of returning life. Mattie was bound up in her father; for her mother dying when she was quite a child, her love had been lavished on her remaining parent. 'She is like the apple of my eye,' he used to say; and to a busybody who asked him one day why he did not marry again, he replied somewhat severely, 'No, I'll never have any woman to come between me and my little Mattie.' Her sister too and brother overcome with grief were tremblingly watching the fruitless efforts of the rescuers.

''Tes all arver, I b'lieve,' incautiously whispered one man to another. Mattie, who had been suppressing her feelings with a great effort up till now, overheard the remark:

'What! my faather gone?' she asked, and fell on his body in an agony of grief. 'Lem me die weth'n' she cried. 'My dear, dear faather. Lem me go to he and mawther. You dear, good faather.' She was fervently kissing his lips, but no sign of life followed. The other sister and brother hung over their father, bitterly crying. It was a pitiful sight. Rough men standing around were freely giving way to grief.

The afternoon was closing in, but still the three orphans hung over the corpse.

'We must git the poor little sauls away,' said a fisherman; ''twill be dark soon now.'

'Come, come,' said an old woman coaxingly, 'doon't a'give way so. Why ted'n as ef yer faather wasn't fit to go. He, dear creatur', es spenden' his Christmas Eve with the Lord.'

'Come in weth me, an' ave some tay. Come, Mattie dear,' said Gracie gently lifting up her sister's head. She quietly obeyed. Then turning her woe-begone face towards the cove, she shuddered, murmuring sadly as if to herself, 'Dear faather, lost, and nearly home!'

This might seem too sad an ending for our little book; but no doubt it will be read by some to whom Yule-tide will come

laden with new sorrow or with memories of old loss, as well as by the festive and light-hearted. Upon such mourners the merry-makings of others will perhaps jar, and they may find it hard to restrain murmurous envy of happier friends. Possibly it will help them to learn that they are not after all outcasts of fortune, and most tried of human kind, if they are reminded that it was thus they sometimes spent Christmas at St Cadge and that Mrs Oliver's tea-party, and pawns, and cakes, and mummers, and carols were only one side of Christmas in Cornwall sixty years ago.

*Having lost my mother who died suddenly this year, this extract for me is especially poignant, and the picture of the orphans on the Cornish beach the more moving.*

## *from*

# Vanishing Cornwall

## DAPHNE DU MAURIER

*Daphne du Maurier died in April 1989 at the age of eighty-one after many happy years living in Cornwall, which she came to regard as home. She first came to Cornwall in 1927 on holiday with her mother and two sisters and she*

*immediately fell in love with the place. Later, when her parents bought a house called Ferryside at Bodinnick, she said, 'From that time, I never wanted to return to London.' From Bodinnick she and her husband, the late Lieutenant General Sir Frederick Browning, and their three children moved to Menabilly House at Par, where some of her most famous novels were written. It was thought that Menabilly was the inspiration for Mandeley in* Rebecca *but she said that in fact the inspiration came from Milton Hall near Peterborough. For over fifty years Daphne du Maurier has been one of the world's best selling authors. The list of her works includes many romantic classics, such as* Frenchman's Creek, Rebecca, Jamaica Inn, *and* My Cousin Rachel. *Many of her works have been filmed, most notably* The Birds *and* Don't Look Now. *This extract from* Vanishing Cornwall, *first published in 1967, captures some of that special flavour of Cornwall, present in so much of her work, as she and her son set off on the trail of a legend that has its origins in a Christmas now lost in the mists of time.*

### The Legend of Penrose

'What remains of the old mansion in Penrose, in Sennen, stands on a low and lonely site at the head of a narrow valley through which a mill-brook winds, with many abrupt turns, for about three miles, thence to Penberth Cove.' These words, from the old book of *Hearthenside Stories*, had imprinted themselves in my mind, for a modern map says nothing of lonely sites or winding brooks, and the red circle I had drawn about the name of Penrose might cover, for all I knew, a caravan camp dumped above a stream.

Here is the trouble when searching for the past. Imagination conjures up bare hills and wilder shores, manors with tall chimneys flanked by courtyards, only to find, when catching

Jamaica Inn at Bolbentor, Cornwall, immortalized by
Daphne du Maurier

up with the present, that rows of houses or perhaps a
filling-station dominate the hill, that a smuggler's cove has
beach-huts and the foundations of a Tudor home are hidden
beneath a stuccoed Victorian villa or modern bungalow.

'We can only drive there and find out,' my son said firmly,
'and if there's nothing left . . .' He shrugged in resignation
and we set forth once again, with maps and field-glasses, to
that 'promontory of slaughter', West Penwith. As we drove,
some fifty miles or more, I told him the story in the same
language as I remembered it, as it was no doubt told in
countless cottages on winter nights before an open hearth in
bygone days, with the rain beating upon the window-panes
outside.

'Long, long ago,' I said, 'some three hundred years or maybe more, there was an ancient family called Penrose, living in the manor house that bore their name in Sennen parish. The country there-abouts was wild and naked, exposed to the salt wind from the sea, and in winter the rain fretted the wheat out of the ground, so that it was washed away and useless, the only land for cultivation being the close places between the hills. The head of the family in those days was Ralph Penrose, who as a young man had led a seafaring life, and when he succeeded to his father's estate so great still was his love for sailing and the sea that he built himself a ship and became what they called then a fair-trader, or, as we say today, smuggler. He was never a pirate, as some of them were, or robbed the poor, but would sail across to France, with his devoted crew, most of them poor relations who could find no better means of living, and then bring back merchandise to Sennen, and distribute it amongst the people in the neighbourhood and members of his own household. He traded for the love of the game, as did his cousin William, as great an adventurer as himself.

'Sorrow came to Ralph one autumn, when his wife died of a fever, and from then onwards he seemed to take a dislike to the land, being at sea more than ever and taking his only son with him, a lad of seven. He would do this even in winter, leaving his estate to be managed by his younger brother John. One winter's night, before the turn of the year, Ralph Penrose was sailing home from France with his ship well-laden, his crew in good heart and his cousin William and his young son aboard, when a gale sprang up some miles south of the Land's End, and the ship struck the dreaded Cowloe rocks and foundered. He and his men, battling with tremendous seas, launched a boat, but this too was overturned, and Ralph, his son, his cousin and his crew were flung into the water. Flares from the foundering ship had warned the household ashore, and John Penrose came down from the manor house to Sennen cove. Standing there, in the darkness and the wind, he heard the cries of the stricken men, and it was later whispered, did nothing for them, but let them drown. Ralph, William, all the crew were lost. The only one to come ashore, mercifully unharmed, was his nephew, the heir, the lad of seven.

'Life changed at Penrose manor after that mournful night. John, appointing himself guardian of his nephew, behaved as if the property was his. The old quiet ways were over, and riotous living took their place. The fisherfolk in Sennen dreaded for the safety of their wives and daughters, who dared not stir from their doors when John Penrose was abroad. Fearing the sea himself he built a larger, stronger craft than ever his brother had owned, and manned it with a captain and a crew whose reputation for evil living excelled even his own, so that now the name of Penrose was not connected with fair trading but with piracy. On winter nights when the villains shunned the sea, John Penrose would invite the captain and his crew to drink with him at the manor, and wild would be the shouting and the laughter, and blazing the torch-lights and the lanterns, as the drunken inmates staggered about the court yard and stumbled in the passages and the hall.

'One winter snow fell upon Sennen, and rumour ran that wolves had been seen on the commons above Penrose. Half crazed with excitement and drink, John Penrose bade his household go in search of them, while he and his boon companion, the skipper of the pirate vessel, stayed within doors, a bottle of brandy on the table between them.

'When the servants returned they called for their young master, the heir, to tell him that the wolves had vanished, but the boy was nowhere to be seen, neither in the house nor in the grounds outside. His uncle and the captain, too drunk to answer questions, murmured that the lad, having gone to join the hunt, would soon return. Once more the steward and the servants went out into the night, across the fields to the cliffs, even down to Sennen cove, where the orphaned boy so often wandered, musing on his father's death. They found no trace of him, neither that night, nor in the light of morning, nor in the days to come. It was assumed that young Penrose, blinded perhaps by the driving snow, and missing his way, had fallen from a cliff into the sea, and drowned there amongst the rocks as his father had before him. The household mourned, but John Penrose, being full master at last, gave himself up to even greater folly than before, spent recklessly, gambled his heritage, and led his band of vagabonds about the countryside, putting the fear of death into all his neighbours. One thing was strange. He took an aversion to the captain of his ship, who, giving no explanation to anyone, relinquished his command and left the district.

'The following winter, on the anniversary of the boy's disappearance, between Christmas and New Year, John Penrose was carousing amongst his cronies when a stranger came into the courtyard of the house, and knocking upon the door asked for hospitality. The steward admitted him, for wanderers often begged shelter at these times, and his master, deep in his cups, ordered that the guest should be shown to his dead brother's room in the old wing. A fire was laid and kindled in the hearth and the steward brought food and drink, and as he placed them before the guest he admitted, shaking his head, that evil days had fallen upon the house. Strange things were seen and heard that never were before, and all since the young heir had been lost twelve months ago. The stranger listened in silence, if silence it could be called, for even in the old wing the sound of revelry came from the hall below.

'The steward left, bidding the guest goodnight. The stranger opened the window which gave onto the side-court and watched the revellers making merry because of the New Year to come, picking ivy, strewing it upon themselves and the cobbles, shouting how some of them would be wedded

before the year was out. Suddenly one of them cried out in fright, pointing to the white wreaths of mist and fog rolling in towards them from the sea. One and all they ran back into the house and slammed the door, and the music and sounds of revelry ceased. The stranger waited, watching the rolling mist.'

Here I was interrupted by my son. 'You're making it up,' he said.

'No,' I said, 'really, I'm not.'

'You must be,' he insisted. 'You're bringing in the fog because of last time, when it came down on us after Madron Well.'

'No,' I told him, 'it's coincidence. The fog is all part of the old story.'

He grunted disbelievingly. 'Well, anyway, go on.'

'The fog came first,' I continued, 'and then, from the same direction, came a sound like the roaring of the sea, yet the sea

was distant a mile or more, and the manor of Penrose set at the valley's head between the hills. The sound of the storm drew nearer, the roar of breakers upon the shore, the rattling of oars shipping into the row-locks, and the splintering of wood and in a moment the breakers themselves tumbled upon the courtyard, bearing upon their crest a long boat filled with crying men, who called out in terror, "Save us . . . save us . . ." The sea was all about the house, curling and green, and the boat of a sudden overturned, spilling her crew, who with white faces and staring eyes sought to save themselves, and sank; but one man, lasting longer than his comrade, looked up at the window where the stranger stood and cried in a loud voice, "William Penrose, arise and avenge the murder of your cousin's son!" Then all was still. There was no more storm and no more sea, no more anguish of drowning men. The court was cobbled as it had been before, and the ivy strewn where the revellers had left it. The mist dissolved.

'The stranger, William Penrose, for it was indeed he, the cousin believed by all in Sennen to be drowned, passed his hand over his eyes. The memory of that terrible night came back to him. How he had dragged himself ashore and wandered, a vagrant, about the countryside unknown to any man, and finally taken ship to a distant land until some instinct within him made him seek out his home, as he had done that night.

'The words rang in his ears. "Avenge the murder of your cousin's son!" He flung himself upon his bed to sleep, and while he slept it seemed to him that the voice of the young boy whispered in his ear, "My uncle bade the captain murder me. I lie beneath the dead tree in the orchard. Dig, and you shall find me. Dig, and place my bones in Sennen churchyard. Dig, and give me peace at last."

'When morning came William Penrose awoke, and seeking out the good steward in his quarters there revealed himself for who he was, swearing the man to secrecy. He said nothing of the fearful revelations of the night before, for he wished first to find, if possible, the murderous captain who had killed his cousin's son. He traced him, after several days, to Plymouth, where the wretched fellow, unfit for further piracy or plotting, tortured by remorse and fear of discovery, lay dying in a lodging-house. When questioned he confessed all, admitting that it was not for gold only that he had killed the boy but because, as a young man, he loved the child's mother, and when she had married Ralph, the devil had entered his heart.

'There, on the lodging-house bed, the captain died, and William returned to his cousin's house. He found the master absent, for since the night of Christmas revelry, so the steward told him, John Penrose had fallen into a fit of melancholy, desiring neither drink nor company, nor had he been seen to smile or raise his head. Together, William and the steward went to the orchard. One tree, amongst the others, was naked white, the branches bare and pointing to the sky. They dug beneath it. Slowly, gently, they lifted the tangled remains of the once lovely boy, the clothes about him stained with blood and mould. They carried him by night to Sennen churchyard and laid him to Christian rest as he had desired, saying nothing to any member of the household, nor to the villagers, out of respect for the once honoured family name.

'When they returned to Penrose they found the door of the malt house below the manor blowing wide, and entering they saw something swaying backwards and forwards from a beam. It was the body of John Penrose. He had hanged himself in the sight of the blasted tree.'

*from*

# The Hound of the Baskervilles

## ARTHUR CONAN DOYLE

*Dartmoor is magnificent; it is one of the last great untouched areas of the country – but beware the weather, which can change here in an instant, from clear skies one moment to swirling mists the next. In winter the cold can penetrate even the warmest of clothing and cut through to the very bone. The famous grey granite prison at Prince-town can look a grim and forbidding place shrouded in mist or with a covering of snow made crisp and brittle by sharp, white frost.*

*It was Dartmoor that Sir Arthur Conan Doyle chose as the setting for his Sherlock Holmes story,* The Hound of the Baskervilles, *a tale of horror and suspense, which makes the ideal read at Christmas, and a book that I return to time and time again.*

*A certain Dr James Mortimer has been to consult the world-famous detective at 221b Baker Street, telling him of the legend of the hound from hell, the curse of the Baskerville family, and explaining his concern for the safety and well-being of the heir to Baskerville Hall, Sir*

# · *A West Country Christmas* ·

*Henry, who is due to arrive shortly from Canada. Holmes, much to Dr Watson's bemusement, plays down his real interest in the case and pretends to be too busy to give the matter his immediate attention, saying that he has to remain in London and cannot afford to take time off to travel to Devon. Dr Mortimer is clearly very disappointed, but accepts Holmes' suggestion that Dr Watson should accompany him and Sir Henry back to the West Country and keep Holmes informed of any developments. Holmes, however, a master of disguise and surprise, arrives on on a cold, crisp winter's evening, when he and Watson meet again . . .*

The last red streaks had faded away in the west and night had settled upon the moor. A few faint stars were gleaming in a violet sky.

Hound Tor, Dartmoor

'One last question, Holmes,' I said, as I rose. 'Surely there is no need of secrecy between you and me. What is the meaning of all this? What is he after?'

Holmes' voice sank as he answered – 'It is murder, Watson – refined, cold blooded, deliberate murder. Do not ask me for particulars. My nets are closing upon him, even as his are upon Sir Henry, and with your help he is already almost at my mercy. There is but one danger which can threaten us. It is that he should strike before we are ready to do so. Another day – two at most – and I have my case complete, but until then guard your charge as closely as ever a fond mother watched her ailing child. Your mission today has justified itself, and yet I could almost wish that you had not left his side – Hark!'

A terrible scream – a prolonged yell of horror and anguish burst out of the silence of the moor. That frightful cry turned the blood to ice in my veins.

'Oh, my God!' I gasped. 'What is it? What does it mean?'

Holmes had sprung to his feet, and I saw his dark, athletic outline at the door of the hut, his shoulders stooping, his head thrust forward, his face peering into the darkness.

'Hush!' he whispered. 'Hush!'

The cry had been loud on account of its vehemence, but it had pealed out from somewhere far off on the shadowy plain. Now it burst upon our ears, nearer, louder, more urgent than before.

'Where is it?' Holmes whispered; and I knew from the thrill of his voice that he, the man of iron, was shaken to the soul. 'Where is it, Watson?'

'There I think.' I pointed into the darkness.

'No, there!'

Again the agonized cry swept through the silent night, louder and much nearer than ever. And a new sound mingled with it, a deep muttered rumble, musical yet menacing, rising and falling like the low, constant murmur of the sea.

The Hound of the Baskervilles

'The hound!' cried Holmes. 'Come, Watson, come! Great heavens, if we are too late!'

He had started running swiftly over the moor, and I had followed at his heels. But now from somewhere among the broken ground immediately in front of us there came one last despairing yell, and then a dull, heavy thud. We halted and listened. Not another sound broke the heavy silence of the windless night.

I saw Holmes put his hand up to his forehead, like a man distracted. He stamped his foot upon the ground.

'He has beaten us, Watson. We are too late.'

'No, no, surely not!'

'Fool that I was to hold my hand. And you, Watson, see what comes of abandoning your charge! But, by Heaven, if the worst has happened, we'll avenge him!'

Blindly we ran through the gloom, blundering against boulders, forcing our way through gorse bushes, panting up hills and rushing down slopes, heading always in the direction whence those dreadful sounds had come. At every rise Holmes looked eagerly round him, but the shadows were thick upon the moor and nothing moved upon its dreary face.

'Can you see anything?'

'Nothing.'

'But, hark, what is that?'

A low moan had fallen upon our ears. There it was again upon our left! On that side a ridge of rocks ended in a sheer cliff, which overlooked a stone-strewn slope. On its jagged face was spread-eagled some dark, irregular object. As we ran towards it the vague outline hardened into a definite shape. It was a prostrate man face downwards upon the ground, the head doubled under him at a horrible angle, the shoulders rounded and the body hunched together as if in the act of throwing a somersault. So grotesque was the attitude that I could not for an instant realize that that moan had been the passing of his soul. Not a whisper, not a rustle, rose now from the dark figure over which we stooped. Holmes laid his hand upon him, and held it up again, with an exclamation of horror. The gleam of the match which he struck shone upon his clotted fingers and upon the ghastly pool which widened slowly from the crushed skull of the victim. And it shone upon something else which turned our hearts sick and faint within us – the body of Sir Henry Baskerville!

There was no chance of either of us forgetting that peculiar ruddy tweed suit – the very one which he had worn on the first morning that we had seen him in Baker Street. We caught the one clear glimpse of it, and then the match flickered and went out, even as the hope had gone out of our souls. Holmes groaned, and his face glimmered white through the darkness.

'The brute! The brute!' I cried, with clenched hands. 'Oh, Holmes, I shall never forgive myself for having left him to his fate.'

'I am more to blame than you, Watson. In order to have my case well rounded and complete, I have thrown away the life of my client. It is the greatest blow which has befallen me in my career. But how could I know – how could I know – that he would risk his life upon the moor in the face of all my warnings?'

'That we should have heard his screams – my God, those screams! – and yet have been unable to save him! Where is this brute of a hound which drove him to his death? It may be lurking among these rocks at this instant. And Stapleton, where is he? He shall answer for this deed.'

'He shall. I will see to that. Uncle and nephew have been murdered – the one frightened to death by the very sight of a beast, which he thought to be supernatural, the other driven to his end in his wild flight to escape from it. But now we have to prove the connection between the man and the beast. Save from what we heard, we cannot even swear to the existence of the latter, since Sir Henry has evidently died from the fall. But, by heavens, cunning as he is, the fellow shall be in my power before another day is past!'

We stood with bitter hearts on either side of the mangled body, overwhelmed by this sudden and irrevocable disaster which had brought all our long and weary labours to so piteous an end. Then, as the moon rose, we climbed to the top of the rocks over which our poor friend had fallen, and from the summit we gazed out over the shadowy moor, half silver and half gloom.

# The Glastonbury Thorn

The story of the Glastonbury Thorn is perhaps well known far beyond Somerset, from where it originates, but nevertheless it bears the retelling as it is very much a part of Christmas and its celebration in the West Country.

There are many legends about holy bushes or trees, each of which is supposed to have grown from a Holy Thorn from Jesus' crucifixion crown. (Indeed, there was just such a Holy Thorn bush at my school in London.) The legend of the Thorn at Glastonbury can be traced back to Joseph of Arimathea, who was responsible for conveying Jesus' body from the cross to the tomb which he had prepared. He was also, according to

# · *A West Country Christmas* ·

THE
GLASTONBURY
THORN

©1977

the legend, a well-off merchant who visited parts of the West Country, trading in tin and lead. In 63 A.D., so the story goes, Joseph was chosen by St Philip to lead a band of twelve men across to Britain and teach the gospel. It would seem that he first landed in either Wales or Barrow Bay in Somerset, but, after an unfriendly welcome, moved on to the kingdom of King Arviragus. The King listened to Joseph but steadfastly refused to be converted from his heathen ways. Instead he offered the disciple land at Ynyswitrin, or Glastonbury, on which to build his church, an offer which Joseph accepted.

Joseph headed for Glastonbury, his mission incomplete. Here his message was greeted with such disbelief and scorn that Joseph prayed for a sign or a miracle to convince them of the truth of the gospel that he was trying to teach. One day, we are told in a tract, his prayers were answered, while climbing Wearyall Hill:

Fixing his pilgrim's staff in the ground, it was no sooner set

75

Sarah Cruwys cutting a sprig of the Glastonbury Thorn in
1988 as the Mayor, Dr Hugh Sharp (right), and Tom
Clark, the Warden of the Thorn, look on

in the earth but just like Aaron's rod it was presently turned
into a blossoming tree, which supernatural miracle made
numerous spectators, who came to see the wonder, be very
attentive to hear his preaching the Gospel, which was
concerning Christ Crucified for the redemption of mankind.

Hence the legend of the Thorn was born. It is supposed to
blossom twice a year – once at Christmas and again at Easter –
in a cluster of small white flowers flecked with pink, and,
although it appears similar to many double-flowering thorns
growing in Britain, it is not a native of this country. It comes
from Palestine, a fact which seems to add authenticity to the
legend.

76

The Glastonbury Thorn, however, has rivals in the West Country. At Clooneaven House at Lynmouth in North Devon there is a thorn bush which is also reputed to burst into flower at Christmas. Similarly, at West Buckland in Somerset there is another thorn with the same properties as at Glastonbury, although this one is supposed to flower on the stroke of midnight on 5 January, or 'Old Christmas'. Here the flowers stay out, so the legend has it, for about ten minutes before returning back into their buds until ready to flower again in the spring.

What none of these 'rivals' can boast, however, is the royal connection that the Glastonbury Thorn has. Traditionally, a gift of a piece of the Thorn has been sent to the royal family for centuries. It is believed that the custom started before the Reformation, and it may have originated with a gift once made to Henry VIII's Vicar General, Thomas Cromwell. In 1929, the vicar of St John's, Glastonbury, the Reverend Lionel Lewis, revived the custom of sending sprigs of the Thorn to the royal family at Christmas.

More recently, the Mayor of Glastonbury has been invited to join the vicar of St John's in sending this token of loyalty and seasonal good wishes to the Queen and the Queen Mother.

The sprigs of the Glastonbury Thorn, it would seem, are greatly appreciated, and appear on the Queen's dining table at Windsor and on the Queen Mother's writing desk at Clarence House, a reminder of a real West Country tradition at Christmas time.

In 1986, the legend of the Glastonbury Thorn was depicted in the commemorative issue of Christmas stamps by the Post Office and so many millions would have seen the thorn tree on the 12p and 13p stamps probably without realizing that it was part of a West Country Christmas.

# Keepen Up O'Chris'mas

## WILLIAM BARNES

*Another of William Barnes' poems now, this time in dialect, so try and get your Dorset tongue round this.*

An' zoo you didden come athirt,
To have zome fun last night: how wer't?
Vor we'd a-work'd wi'all our might
To scour the iron things up bright,
An' brush'd an' scrubb'd the house all drough;
An' brought in vor a brand, a plock

# · A West Country Christmas ·

O' wood so big's an uppen-stock,
An' hung a bough o'misseltoo,
An' axed a merry friend or two,
   To keepen up o'Chris'mas.

An' there wer wold an' young; an' Bill,
Soon after dark, stalk'd up vrom mill.
An' when he wer a-comen near,
He whissled loud vor me to hear;
The roun' my head my frock I roll'd,
An' stood in orcha'd like a post,
To meake en think I wer a ghost.
But he wer up to't, an' did scwold
To vind me stannen in the cwold,
   A-keepen up o'Chris'mas.

We played at forfeits, an' we spun
The trencher roun', an' meade such fun!
An' had a geame o'dree-cead loo,
An' then begun to hunt the show.
An' all the wold vo'k zitten near,
A-chatten roun' the vier pleace,
Did smile in woone another's feace,
An' sheake hands wi' hearty cheer,
An' let their hands spill their beer,
   A-keepen up o'Chris'mas.

*from*

# Christmas in Cornwall Sixty Years Ago

## MRS JOHN BONHAM

### Ghosts

Every village in Cornwall had its own particular ghosts, and St Cadge was no exception to the rule, its ghost appearing as was meet and right, one Christmas Eve. But we must go back a few years in order to make things plain.

Billy Bottrell and Betty Coade were a quiet-going pair during their courtship. Betty, who lived in farm service, always said that once a week, namely Sunday, was often enough for any decent young woman to see her 'shiner'; and no mistress, we may be sure, would dispute that matter with her. Folks said Billy was not very bright, and that, Betty, fairly good-looking and a capital servant, might do better; but she was pleased with her choice, and that settled it.

Christmas Eve, the day before the wedding, had arrived, and Billy in great glee clapped his hands, grinned, and leaped about like one demented. 'Ah!' he explained exultingly to

some friends, 'I'm Billy Bottrell to-day, I shall be William Coade to-morrow.' His brain was in a whirl, and he had somehow mixed things up.

Billy and Betty began house-keeping in a long, low thatched building containing only one large room. There was a lovely view of St Cadge cove and cliffs from the cottage, though doubtless the inmates thought little of that.

The surplus vegetables from their large garden partly provided a pig, which they would feed up for killing. Billy's idea of feeding a pig was a novel one, for it had a feast one day, and a fast the next, so as to make streaky pork, as he used to say.

Time went on till the cottage swarmed with children. Betty had decent ideas, and she worried about so many sleeping in one room that served for every purpose. She soon conceived a plan, brought in a few laths and some thin lengths of wood, and then with her own hands fixed up two or three partitions to form cubicles. These partitions she covered with news-papers, begged from the respectable farmers for miles around, for in those days papers were scarce, costing fourpence half-penny each.

After great exertions she managed to secure a little privacy for the elder children, though her achievement only consisted of a very frail structure; so one morning, when there was a strong southerly wind blowing directly against Betty's door, and Mr Collins, wishing to speak to Billy, lifted the latch and opened it, a blast swept through the interior, and the papered partitions rattled and quivered like aspen-leaves.

'Aw! my dear saul!' cried Betty in great alarm; 'shut the doer, quick – shut'n, ar my screens will be down all of a heap.'

Billy's wages were small, but the large family managed somehow to get along on them, supplemented by a little smuggling job.

In the course of time the elder boys went into farm service and times grew somewhat better.

One Christmas Eve just seventeen years after Billy's wedding, Jackman the eldest boy came home very ill; and Billy thinking him in danger rode off on a borrowed horse for the doctor, who prescribed, gave Betty her orders and left.

Mother and father passed an exciting day, and as the boy now quietly slept, they left him in charge of his eldest sister and hurried down to the 'White Goose' to have a little drop before the house was closed.

Young Collins, and his friend Joe Bennett, always ready for any fun, listened while the story of Jackman's sudden illness was related for the good of every one in the kitchen, and then the two young men slipped out. Their plans were soon formed, and both creeping under an old hedge, that near the ground had been dug out, they waited in a crouching position, their backs to the road, and each with a white garment drawn over the extremity nearest to any passer-by. In a few minutes they heard footsteps coming up the hill.

'Wha's that, Betty, up theere in the 'edge?' asked Billy tremblingly.

'Wheere Billy?'

'Why, up theere – look.'

'Law, whatever es et? Why, 'tes aw tooken, Billy, Jackman'll die, I knaw aw will. They're ghoostes.'

'No, no, Betty,' he replied reassuringly, though trembling himself with fear, 'they're two white pigs,' and he approached cautiously, feeling before him with his stick, but still keeping at some distance. 'Aw hooay – aw hooay,' he cried out to the pigs.

The young men, after allowing him to call and beat his stick on the ground for a minute or two, without in the least altering the position of their bodies, hopped out of the hedge, and to the horror of the frightened couple hopped away down the hill. And such ghostly sights they looked in the partial darkness that Betty in great distress cried out:

'Aw, Billy, my dear boy'll die. Iss aw will, thus aw tooken chul tha's what that es.'

They stood riveted to the spot with fear. Meanwhile the merry youths were no sooner out of sight, than, scampering through the village, they climbed some hedges, ran up the fields, and planted themselves, white backs outwards, near a path along which the couple had to pass to get to their cottage.

At last, partially recovered from their terrible fright, Billy and Betty came slowly up the hill, talking quietly and solemnly. They got over the stile, and there, before them, was the strange vision once more!

'Oh! my goodness guide me, Billy, what shall es do? Theere's the ghoostes agen. Oh! wheere shall I go? Lem me shut my eyes. Oh! Billy, catch hawld of me – Oh! Now we do knaw 'tes two ghoostes 'cause they was down the bottom of the hill jest now, an' now they're up'long here.'

The ghosts once more went hop, hop, down the field, when the horrified couple rushed wildly one after the other, Betty screaming at the top of her voice, and on reaching the cottage, forgetting Jackman, she beat wildly on the door, arousing the poor boy from his peaceful sleep; and then she sank down on the floor and almost fainted away.

The tale of the two ghosts seen on Christmas Eve went the round of St Cadge and its neighbourhood, and was told, not always without exaggeration of its horrors, to many a shuddering circle round the Christmas fire when the carol singing was over: but the ghosts themselves laughed in their sleeves, and kept their secret for years.

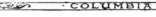

# The Tradition of the Yule Log

A roaring log-fire forms part of everybody's romantic image of Christmas, and the Yule Log has a firm place in West Country tradition. The custom of bringing it to the house and its burning varies from county to county. In Charles Henry Poole's *Customs, Superstitions and Legends of the County of Somerset* it is recorded that:

> The burning of the ashen-faggot on Christmas Eve is an ancient ceremony transmitted to us from the Scandinavians, who at their feast of Juul, were accustomed to kindle huge bonfires in honour of Thor. The faggot is composed of ashen sticks, hooped round with bands of the same tree, nine in number. When placed on the fire, fun and jollity commence – master and servant are now all on an equal footing. Sports begin – jumping in sacks, diving in the water for apples, and many other innocent games engage the attention of the rustics. Every time the bands crack by reason of the heat of the fire, all present are supposed to drink liberally of cider or egg-hot, a mixture of cider, eggs, etc. The reason why ash is selected in preference to any other timber is, that tradition assigns it as wood with which Our Lady kindled a fire in order to wash her new born Son.

It was traditional to kindle the faggot with a cinder from last year's Yule Log and the fire would then burn throughout the festive season, bringing light and warmth to the whole house. It was believed that the log had to burn for at least twelve hours in order to bring good luck to the household. In Devon, each of the youngest members of the family would choose one of the binds before the ashen faggot was lit. During the burning, whoever's bind burned through first, would, so it was believed, be the first to marry. The following is an eye-witness account of the tradition from the first half of the last century:

> I was present on Christmas Eve, 1836, in the Old Torwood Manor House, Torquay, when the ashen faggot was prepared and burnt. It was made in the farmyard and was bound together by as many binds of withe as possible. When ready, it was drawn to the house by four oxen, as required by custom, although one ox would easily do the work. Then it was transported to and placed on the blazing hearth. Cards and other amusements occupied the young members of the very large party, while the seniors talked of old times. All, however, were watching for the fate of the 'binds' which, one after another burnt through and gave way, whereupon a demand for another gallon of cider was at once met by the farmer.

In 1878, local records indicate how widespread the custom of the ashen faggot was, it being 'observed at 32 farms and cottages in Ashburton postal district'. It is from this Devon parish that another first-hand account comes, describing a macabre variation on the theme of burning the faggot:

> It was usual when the fire was well lighted and the wood beginning to crack, to place the youngest child of the

THE YULE LOG

household on the faggot. The length of time the child stayed there was regarded by the old people as a sign of future bravery, or otherwise.

However, in common with other versions of the ceremony, 'After supper, the amusements of the evening consisted of music, songs, story telling and if possible, dancing, as well as an almost unlimited quantity of cider, apples and nuts.' How different from the modern-day Christmas entertainments!

The Yule Log tradition was also maintained in Cornwall

87

and in this letter, written in 1910, Stanley John Denner remembers the part that the Yule Log played in his family Christmas:

We have kept up the custom as long as I can remember and my grandfather always kept it. My brothers and I went to the woodstack and selected a big log. We put two sticks under it and each taking an end, (there were four of us), carried it in. We put the log into the fireplace and put fire against it. Into the fire we put a fragment of last year's log, which helps to light the new. It is the custom to keep a fragment of last year's log, which helps to light that of next year. If this were not done, old folks would think that their house would catch on fire. I do not believe this super-stition, but one year the fragment that we had saved was accidentally burnt, and our chimney caught fire the same year. I might add that, instead of 'Yule Log' my grandfa-ther called it 'The Christmas Braun'. I have never heard it called that by anyone outside this Parish. The log burned well and we could not sit with comfort within two yards of it that night. I remember one log which burned all the rest of the week.

In some parts of Cornwall the Yule Log was called 'The Mock', whereas in Dorset in was often called 'The Christmas Braund'.

It's sad to reflect that, with the advent of central heating, smaller fireplaces and grates which cannot accommodate the traditional Yule Log, the custom is not as widely celebrated as it once was. Nowadays it's likely that the only Yule Log in the house will be a chocolate-covered Swiss roll with a festive robin and a dusting of sugar, representing the winter snows, on the top!

# Yule Log

## ROBERT HERRICK

*Robert Herrick was born in London in 1591, and went to
St John's College in Cambridge, where he began writing
poetry. He returned to London, and, in 1629, following
the death of his mother, he moved to Dean Prior in Devon.
This is his version of the Yule Log tradition, recording not
only the custom itself, but also a flavour of the great
celebrations surrounding it.*

Come, bring with a noise,
My merrie, merrie boyes,
The Christmas Log to the firing;
While my good Dame, she
Bids you all be free;
And drink to your hearts' desiring.

With last yeeres brand
Light the new block, and
For good successe in his spending,
On your Psaltries play,
That sweet luck may
Come while the log is a-teending.

Drink now the strong Beere,
Cut the white loaf here,
The while the meat is a-shredding;
For the rare Mince-Pie
And the Plums stand by
To fill the paste that's a-kneading.

# The Reminder

## THOMAS HARDY

*It's not difficult to conjure up a picture of that marvellous
man of Dorset literature, Thomas Hardy, sitting by the
fireside at Christmas time as the flickering light from the
fireplace draws shadows on the walls — an atmosphere
perfectly captured in this poem.*

While I watch the Christmas blaze
Paint the room with ruddy rays,
Something makes my vision glide
To the frosty scene outside.

There, to reach a rotting berry,
Toils a thrush — constrained to very
Dregs of food by sharp distress,
Taking such with thankfulness.

*90*

Why, O starving bird, when I
One day's joy would justify,
And put misery out of view,
Do you make me notice you?

Reconstruction of Thomas Hardy's study in Dorchester
County Museum

*from*

# Linhay on the Downs

## HENRY WILLIAMSON

*Henry Williamson was born on 1 December 1895 at Brockley in Kent. Having served in the army during the Great War he worked for a period as a journalist on London newspapers before driving to the West Country on his motor bike and eventually settling at Georgeham in North Devon, where he remained for the rest of his life and where he is now buried.*

*His love and observation of the countryside and rural life led to his writing more than a dozen books, the best-known of which is* Tarka the Otter. *Besides this, he wrote a host of articles, stories and companion novels to* Tarka, *such as his chronicle of country life,* Linhay on the Downs, *from which this seasonal extract, 'The Yule Log', is taken.*

Since Michaelmas the Yule Log has been propped against the walling of the hump-backed bridge over the river, which runs less than a hundred yards away from my cottage door. A small spate brought the log down one day, and the boys and I hauled it out with a lasso. It weighs about one and a half hundred-weight, and is of yew.

Many times have I wondered if it were not too good for burning: if that salmon-pink wood, stronger than oak, should not be reserved for table legs.

A crack running by a twist in the stick finally decided me. There stands the Yule Log, which we shall drag into the sitting-room the day after tomorrow – Christmas Eve.

The small children are excited, and have been rehearsing in make-believe for days. Only this morning Charlie the black cat ate three-year-old Margaret's yoolug – a piece of bacon rind on a string.

It is difficult to remember all the Christmastides of the last few years – there was a happy one up in Rhode Island, when in the daytime we skated on the lakes where herrings had spawned and went to a dance at Fall River at night – another with the Navvies' Battalion in Halton Park, Buckinghamshire, when the P.M.C., a major (recently a sergeant-major, and a proper old buck navvy before the war) gave the Officers' Mess roast beef, saying it was good enough for anyone, and turkeys were only for fops; and he made his subalterns eat the fat too, (he also knocked down defaulting privates in the guard room), but that was long ago – and, yes, there was the flat and lifeless Christmas after the Armistice, when colour and movement had gone from the only world we knew.

Best of all was the strange and beautiful Christmas of 1914, when we made friends with the Saxons of the 133rd Regiment opposite us under the Messines Hill; when in the frosty moonlight of Christmas Eve we strolled about in No-man's-land, talking and listening to the carols sung in German, only forty yards away and later watching with indescribable feelings the candle-lit Christmas tree they planted on their parapet. And the great white star rising from the east, over their lines, which some of us thought must be a light on a pole, it was so bright.

That time had a dream-like quality for my eighteen-year-old self. Many of us, German and English, longed, and even prayed voicelessly, that its good will and kindness should extend and deepen, until no war spirit remained. Alas! It was not realizable – then.

Why should not this Christmas be the best one has known?

The children are beginning to be human beings, with their own personalities, and therefore as companions they are stimulating. Also, we are looking forward as eagerly to our guests' coming as, we hope, they are eagerly anticipating their arrival. It had been fun arranging the bedrooms, and finding odd corners for camp beds.

And the walks we shall have, whatever the weather, on the high ground of Exmoor and in the lanes, with their tall beechen hedges! The blazing of wood fires on open hearths shall greet us when we return, pleasantly tired, to sip tea made from the black iron kettle hanging on its lapping crook from the chimney bar.

I have got a spruce fir, with all its roots; it is set in an oak tub, for later planting-out in the hilltop field. The sapling shall not be murdered; it shall, after Christmas, join the company of its brethren below Windwhistle Spinney. Late on Christmas Eve, when the children are lying excitedly awake upstairs, or breathing sweetly in sleep, we and our friends will deck its branches with shimmering delights. Then into the cupboard under the stairs, until the afternoon party.

Of course everyone will hang out a stocking. And of course Father Christmas will fill each stocking, and everyone will sit at the long refectory table for breakfast. On one side the children, graded according to size, from the gipsy-dark Margaret to the speedwell-eyed Ann – on the other ourselves, the so-called adults, watching happy faces over the table.

Afterwards a two-mile walk across park and fields to church. On the way we shall peer over the parapet of the bridge to see if any of the spawning salmon are visible.

And I shall show my friends the ant-hill beside the river where every travelling otter scratches and rolls, a small hillock very green in spring with many fishbone fragments that nourish the root grasses.

Before the church service everyone greets everyone else in voices that are neither loud nor yet subdued. Contrast is the salt of life; and, after the singing of the good old hymns, we shall return in an amazingly short time to see the turkey turning slowly on the jack-spit by the hearth. And what a fire! The wood for it has been selected and matured for several years. Pine, for the resinous scents; oak for body; elm for its majestic white ash; alder for its charcoal – the flames of these woods will blend and be thrown out by the bulk of the yew-wood back-brand.

The twin rows of human cormorants will perch themselves along our table, I shall refuse to carve, corks will pop with bubble of grape and ginger; the lighted pudding, set with holly sprigs, will come in, with the mince pies, to be eyed with lessening enthusiasm except by the rows of brighter faces. Who will want figs, dates or nuts? Then for the crackers.

There will be ping-pong, skittles, bagatelle, lead-horse racing, crown-and-anchor, and maybe (since Harold is of the party) the three card trick. And those of us who have realized the poise and harmony between life and death will meet in my writing-room, to listen and to think as the voice of the King, symbol of our hopes for our brother men and neighbours, speaks around the earth.

Yes: this Christmas, I hope, will be proper. Windles, the eldest boy, has just come in to tell me he has seen Father Christmas's reindeer! They were going up the path to Bremridge Wood . . . or else they were the red deer from Exmoor, driven down by the hard weather. Which were they, Dad?

Quick Windles, tell the others what you've seen! Christmas! Christmas!

# The Play's the Thing

The origins of the Mummers' Plays, traditionally performed at Christmas time, are lost in folklore. The plays can be likened to a medieval miracle play and the word 'mummer' is probably derived from the Danish word 'mumme', which doesn't mean 'silent', but rather 'to be disguised with a mask'. The plays became so popular and the performances so riotous during the reign of Henry VIII that a proclamation was issued banning those taking part from wearing masks, fearing that the disguises induced frenzy in the audiences. However the masks were abandoned and costumes substituted and the performances continued much the same as before.

The plot of the plays stemmed from a well-known pageant based on the legend of St George which had been performed in the fourteenth and fifteenth centuries. The cast list included St George himself, a Turkish knight, old Father Christmas and a doctor. Following the historical influences of the crusades, St George fights the Turkish knight and after a fierce battle triumphs in the end, representing the victory of the Christians over paganism. Although the main characters remain basically the same, attempts were made to make the play more topical, and over the centuries figures like the Duke of Wellington, Napoleon and Nelson were introduced into the cast.

A variation from this practice, however, was recorded in 1908 by E.E. Belch:

Coming on Christmas Eve like the mummers to Stourton, Wiltshire, was the Christmas Bull, having features similar to those of the old Hobby Horse commonly to be seen from St Thomas's Day to Epiphany, in former times. The head of the bull, with large bottle eyes, large horns, and lolling tongue, was supported and manipulated by a man stooping over a broomstick and hidden by sacking; the head was attached to one end of the broomstick and the tail was a piece of rope. The bull was operated so as to knock at the door of a house with its horns, and if allowed in, chased the youngsters of the family. Even in the surrounding districts, the Christmas Bull is unknown and I have never heard of the custom being practised in other parts of the country.

In Cornwall, this song, which is sung to the tune of 'The Grand Old Duke of York', is used by the Christmas Mummers as an introduction:

> Oh, a-mumming we will go, will go,
> Oh, a-mumming we will go,
> With bright cockades all in our hats
> We'll make a gallant show.

A Cornish play included these lines by Father Christmas:

> As I lay on my silent bed,
> I dreamt my only son was dead.
> Thou cruel monster, what hast thou done?
> Thou'st ruined and killed my only son.

In Devon, as in other parts of the West Country, the Mummers' Plays were performed by local people who would get together a few weeks or days before Christmas, to

practise. They would start to give public performances from Christmas Eve onwards at any venue that was suitable such as the village green or square, the public houses or the large estate manor-houses. Following the performance there would be a collection.

The performance of these plays has now largely died out, although at the village of Marshfield in Avon, people travel from miles around on Boxing Day to see the Marshfield Paper Boys perform. In spite of the efforts of the then vicar of Marshfield, Revd Canon Trotman, whose family performed the play themselves, it ceased to be staged in about 1890. In 1932, however, it was revived by Violet Alford, a well-known folklorist who, by talking to those who had performed the play in their youth, managed to reconstruct it and revive the tradition which has continued ever since. The name given to the Mummers, or Players, comes from their costumes, which are made of newspaper stuck on to a course gown or cloak.

Because these plays were passed down from one generation to the next by word of mouth it was easy for the 'script' to be lost as it was seldom recorded on paper. Here, however, is a version of a Mummers' Play, which gives a flavour of how it may have sounded, although the printed text cannot, of course, convey the scope for ad-libbing, topical changes, and the ham acting, nor for the overriding sense of fun and sheer enjoyment felt by both the Mummers and their audience. A great shame that the tradition, like so many of these old customs, is no longer with us in the West Country.

'Here come I, old Father Christmas, welcome or welcome not, I hope old Father Christmas will never be forgot.
Room, room, brave gallants, give us room!
We've come to show our acting on this Christmas time.'

'Here come I, Saint George the valiant knight,
To slay the Turkish Knight I'm come to fight,
'Twas I that brought the Dragon to the slaughter,
And won the King of Egypt's fairest daughter.'

'Here come I, the Turkish Knight,
From the Turkish Land to fight,
I'll fight Saint George, with courage bold,
And if his blood be hot, I'll make it cold.'

The 'stage directions' tell us that a terrible and furious fight
follows between Saint George and the Turkish Knight (sometimes Napoleon would attack Saint George as well) but the
English Knight would be victor and, standing over his defeated
enemies, would proclaim:

These men have had some deep and deadly wounds,
I fear they'll never wish to fight again;
Is there a doctor to be found,
Who can cure these men of their deep and deadly wound?

And, as if by magic, a doctor appears:

DOCTOR        Yes, Saint George, there is a doctor to be
              found,
              Able to cure these men of their deep and
              deadly wound.

ST GEORGE     What are thy travels Doctor?

DOCTOR        Sir, I've travelled through Italy, Ireland,
              Germany and Spain,
              And if these champions' heads are off,
              I'll put them on again.

ST GEORGE     Try thy skill doctor.

After an examination and much shaking of the head, the doctor then administers a potion or pill which speedily produces a miraculous recovery in his patients, who are on their feet again in no time. Good has won over evil, for there is great power in the doctor's healing hands. Once again all is well with the world and peace reigns. After all, it is Christmas!

*from*

# Hercule Poirot's Christmas

## AGATHA CHRISTIE

*Agatha Christie was born in Torquay in Devon in 1890 and ever after had a strong attachment to the West Country. She came by her famous surname when she married Archie Christie on Christmas Eve in 1914 and during the Great War she worked as a nurse in Torquay Hospital. It was here that she started to write detective stories. Her first to be published,* The Mysterious Affair at Styles, *which was completed at a hotel on Dartmoor, earned her the princely sum of twenty-five pounds and introduced the character of Hercule Poirot, the Belgian detective, to the world.*

# · *A West Country Christmas* ·

*She divorced Christie, although she continued to write under the name and married Max Mallowan. Together they bought Greenway House on the banks of the River Dart in Devon in 1939. The thirty-three acres cost them £6,000. More of Greenway later . . . for now, here is a timely warning from a particularly seasonal tale of intrigue and suspense.*

'Nothing like a wood fire,' said Colonel Johnson as he threw on an additional log and then drew back his chair nearer the blaze. 'Help yourself,' he added, hospitably calling attention to the tantalus and siphon that stood near his guest's elbow.

The guest raised a polite hand in negation. Cautiously he edged his own chair nearer to the blazing logs, though he was of the opinion that the opportunity for roasting the soles of one's feet (like some mediaeval torture) did not offset the cold draught that swirled round the back of the shoulders.

Colonel Johnson, chief constable of Middleshire, might be of the opinion that nothing could beat a wood fire, but Hercule Poirot was of the opinion that central heating could and did every time!

'Amazing business, that Cartwright case,' remarked the host reminiscently. 'Amazing man! Enormous charm of manner. Why, when he came here with you, he had us all eating out of his hand.'

He shook his head.

'We'll never have anything like that case!' he said. 'Nicotine poisoning is rare, fortunately.'

'There was a time when you would have considered all poisoning un-English,' suggested Hercule Poirot. 'A device of foreigners! Unsportsmanlike!'

'I hardly think we can say that,' said the chief constable. 'Plenty of poisoning by arsenic – probably a good deal more than has ever been suspected.'

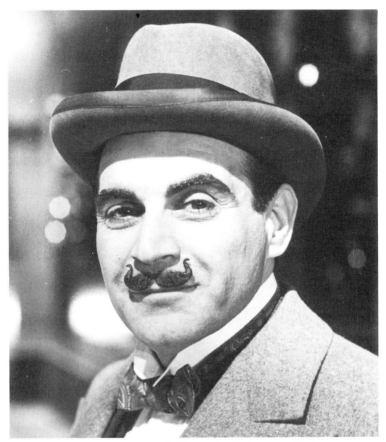

David Suchet as Hercule Poirot in the London Weekend
Television series

'Always an awkward business, a poisoning case,' said
Johnson. 'Conflicting testimony of the experts – then doctors
are usually so extremely cautious in what they say. Always a
difficult case to take to a jury. No, if one *must* have a murder
(which heaven forbid!) give me a straightforward case. Some-

thing where there's no ambiguity about the cause of death.'

Poirot nodded.

'The bullet wound, the cut throat, the crushed-in skull? It is there your preference lies?'

'Oh don't call it preference, my dear fellow. Don't harbour the idea that I *like* murder cases! Hope I never have another. Anyway we ought to be safe enough during your visit.'

Poirot began modestly: 'My reputation —'

But Johnson had gone on.

'Christmas-time,' he said 'Peace, goodwill — and all that kind of thing. Goodwill all round.'

Hercule Poirot leaned back in his chair. He joined his finger tips. He studied his host thoughtfully.

He murmured: 'It is, then, your opinion that Christmas-time is an unlikely season for crime?'

'That's what I said.'

'Why?'

'Why?' Johnson was thrown slightly out of his stride. 'Well as I've just said — season of good cheer, and all that.'

Hercule Poirot murmured. 'The British, they are so sentimental!'

Johnson said stoutly: 'What if we are? What if we do like the old ways, the old traditional festivities? What's the harm?'

'There is no harm. It is all most charming! But let us for a moment examine the *facts*. You have said that Christmas is a season of good cheer. That means, does it not, a lot of eating and drinking? It means, in fact, the *over-eating*! And with the over-eating comes the irritability!'

'Crimes,' said Colonel Johnson, 'are not committed from irritability.'

'I'm not so sure! Take another point. There is, at Christmas, a spirit of goodwill. It is, as you say, "the thing to do". Old quarrels are patched up, those who have disagreed consent to agree once more, even if it is only temporarily.'

Johnson nodded.

'Bury the hatchet, that's right.'

Poirot pursued his theme: 'And families now, families who have been separated throughout the year, assemble once more together. Now under these conditions, my friend, you must admit that there will occur a great deal of strain. People who do not feel amiable are putting great pressure on themselves to appear amiable! There is at Christmas-time a great deal of hypocrisy, honourable hypocrisy, hypocrisy undertaken *"pour le bon motif"*, *c'est entendu*, but nevertheless hypocrisy.'

'Well I shouldn't put it quite like that myself,' said Colonel Johnson doubtfully.

Poirot beamed upon him.

'No, no. It is I who am putting it like that, not *you*. I am pointing out to you that under these conditions – mental strain, physical malaise – it is highly probable that dislikes that were before merely mild and disagreements that were trivial might suddenly assume a more serious character. The result of pretending to be a more amiable, a more forgiving, a more high-minded person than one really is has sooner or later the effect of causing one to behave as a more disagreeable, a more ruthless and an altogether more unpleasant person than is actually the case! If you dam the stream of natural behaviour, *mon ami*, sooner or later the dam bursts and a cataclysm occurs!'

# Christmas in the Garden with Agatha Christie

## FRANK LAVIN

*Many years ago, while living in London, my parents took us all for our family Christmas treat to see Agatha Christie's* The Mousetrap. *To this day, I can remember it well. At the curtain-call there was an appeal to the audience not to let on 'who done it', and my lips have remained sealed. I thought that this would be the closest that I ever came to Agatha Christie, but many years later, after having moved to the West Country, our paths 'crossed again' in the shape of Frank Lavin.*

*I first met Frank when producing a programme for BBC Radio Devon — a local version of the well-known* Gardeners' Question Time, *which we called* How Does Your Garden Grow? *The format was the same as the Radio Four version, hosted by a local horticultural society, whose members put questions to a panel of gardening experts. The first programme in the series included Frank Lavin on the panel. He was introduced by the chairman as having been Agatha Christie's gardener, and therefore qualified to shed some light on the audience's gardening mysteries.*

*In fact, for over thirty years, from July 1954 until the end of March 1988, Frank worked as Gardens and Estate Manager at Greenway, Agatha Christie's home near the River Dart in South Devon. A quiet self-effacing man, he didn't really make much of having worked for one of the most famous writers of all time. When compiling* A West Country Christmas, *I contacted Frank again and asked him to recall his work at Greenway and what it was like at Christmas time.*

My job was to manage the estate and to work up a tree and shrub business in the areas which were originally vegetable and fruit gardens, so as to defray expenses. Summer was actually the most important time of the year when family and friends were more likely to congregate and a comprehensive programme of fruit and vegetables was required, particularly peaches and nectarines from the one hundred and twenty foot long greenhouse built early in the century.

When Agatha Christie was at Greenway, with her husband Sir Max Mallowan, at Christmas there would be very little garden produce provided, just root vegetables such as potatoes, parsnips and carrots.

On Christmas Eve she and Sir Max, and probably her daughter Mrs Hicks with Mr Hicks, and Matthew Prichard (Mrs Hicks' son by her first marriage) would come into the gardens to wish all the staff 'A Merry Christmas' and to give us each a token present, and to me, in addition, a signed copy of her latest book. Christmas was a quiet occasion and as far as I can remember their Christmases were mostly family affairs with old established friends.

It was also my routine to see that my staff brushed all the woodland paths and the main drive of leaves, and this job

would be left until a week before Christmas, as only by that time had they all fallen from the trees. A plentiful supply of logs always had to be available and she was most particular that these were dry, which entailed felling, splitting and drying suitable trees at least a year previously. That's probably my chief memory of Christmas at Greenway, the home of Agatha Christie, where I worked for so many years.

Frank Lavin with Agatha Christie after success at the Brixham Summer Flower Show thirty years ago (Frank says he looks a little different now!)

# West Country Sayings, Customs and Beliefs

It is said in Cornwall that, 'on Christmas Eve the fairies meet at the bottom of the mine and perform a mass in celebration of the birth of Christ'. Also on Christmas Eve, 'the neck or last sheaf or armful of corn cut in the harvest field and allowed to hang from the ceiling in the farmhouse kitchen, from harvest time until Christmas Eve was taken down and given to the cattle'.

Staying with livestock, it used to be a common practice to bleed horses, cows, oxen and other animals at Christmas time as it was thought that periodical bleeding was good for the health and staying power of working farm animals. In Wiltshire it was said:

> If you bleed your nag on St Stephen's Day,
> He'll work your wark for ever and aye.

Here is one of my favourite superstitions. It comes from Devon, and was recorded by Sarah Hewett in 1900: 'An unmarried girl who desires to learn something of her prospects in marriage goes to the door of the fowlhouse on Christmas Eve, and taps it smartly. If a hen first cackles, the girl's future

is not encouraging but if a cock crows first, the girl, it was believed, would be married before the end of the year.' Unhappily there are no records of how successful this method of forecasting was, but I am sure that if the cock crew, marriage before the end of the year was not meant literally: otherwise it would leave little time to celebrate Christmas before embarking upon the wedding breakfast!

In Somerset it is recorded that on Christmas Eve the festivities would include a feast of hot cakes and nuts, washed down with a drink made up of mulled or warmed ale and spiced roast apples. The cake found favour in Cornwall too, as we learn from the *English Illustrated Magazine* for December 1903: 'In days gone by, every Cornish housewife provided "the Christmas" or the Christmas cake for her household. This was a small saffron or currant cake for presentation on Christmas Eve, to every member of the family and to each guest and the custom was for everybody to taste everybody else's cake by way of good fellowship. This practice is nearly out of fashion but was in evidence last year in some cottage homes near Redruth.'

Decorations formed as much a part of Christmas in times gone by as they do now. Mistletoe, for instance, can be traced back to the Druids, who were convinced that the plant had magicial properties. A parasite chiefly found on oak and apple trees, the Druids called it a 'Curer of all Ills'. They considered that the trees on which it grew were sacred, and that the birds which visited their branches were messengers from the gods. When mistletoe was required for a religious ceremony, it was gathered with great care by a priest, who used a golden sickle to remove it.

Devonians believe that their county was cursed by ancient Druid fathers, who had decreed that mistletoe should not grow there. There is no record to explain this belief but there is an account of a gentleman who possessed an orchard, one half of which lay in Devon, and the other half in Somerset, the

division of the two counties being marked by a deep ditch. On the Devon side of the ditch, the apple trees were free of mistletoe, whereas on the Somerset side the parasite grew in great abundance. Every effort that he made to cultivate it on the trees in Devon failed.

Perhaps it was this 'curse' on mistletoe in Devon which led to the kissing bush being a substitute decoration, often found in poorer homes. The kissing bush was a small furze bush which was dipped in water, powdered with flour and studded with holly berries. The bush wouldn't be hung from the ceiling as mistletoe was, but would be planted in a decorated flowerpot. The kissing bush was the forerunner of the Christmas tree, which was German in origin and made popular by Queen Victoria.

Long before Christmas was celebrated, however, evergreens were used in the winter for decorating sacred places. The holly, one of the most popular evergreens, was originally used at the ancient-Roman festival of Saturn, which took place in about the third week of December. It would seem that the custom was adopted by the early Christians at Rome, who introduced the use of evergreens in the decoration of churches and houses at the time of year which came to be celebrated as Christmas. Since then, holly, rosemary, laurel, bay or bay laurel, ivy, box, fir, yew and mistletoe have all been used at one time or another for the Christmas decoration of homes, market crosses and public places. Fir, ivy, yew and mistletoe have also been used for decorating churches, despite disfavour from some quarters.

At one time, a candle used to be lit on Christmas Eve and every night following till the twelve days of Christmas were over. In 1884, we read that:

A children's game of dancing round the candles is still in vogue at Penryn, at Christmas, but not I think throughout

Cornwall. A basket is filled with sand and candles painted over are stuck on it. The basket is put on the floor and the candles are lighted, then the children dance round the basket, the girls first and then the boys, all singing. This is possibly a vestige of the ancient fire rites of the winter solstice.

Of course there's also the custom of taking down the Christmas decorations and of burning the evergreens on the fire on New Year's Eve. New Year itself has several superstitions attached to it, for example: 'It is unlucky to continue the knitting of a stocking into the New Year,' and, 'To take a silver coin out of the house during the night of New Year's Eve, to hide it, and to take it into the house the next morning, is believed to ensure a supply of money during the coming year.' This is something that I must try, because – who knows? – there may be a lot more to these old sayings, beliefs and customs than meets the eye!

# A Devon Country Christmas

The following is based on a BBC Radio programme which I compiled for BBC Radio Devon, and was broadcast at Christmas time in 1988. The idea of the programme was to look back at the

ways in which Christmas had changed over the years in the county, as opposed to how it is celebrated today. When originally broadcast, the programme produced quite a number of letters from listeners saying how many memories it had evoked for them and in the hope that it will do the same for you, it is re-produced in part here.

We start with Mabel Mudge, or Aunt Mabel, as she is known throughout Devon. Aunt Mabel, who is reckoned to be the oldest landlady in the country, has run The Drewe Arms at Drewsteignton since 1919 and she's in no doubt that Christmas today is a very different kind of affair from when she was younger. 'It's different now to what it was', she says. 'A lot of them didn't have the money to throw about and do the things that they can do today. Oh no, it was completely different.'

James Robertson is an author who now lives and works in Somerset. He has written a series of very funny books, all under the same title of *Any Fool Can be* . . . (. . . *a Dairy Farmer*, . . . *a Pig Farmer*, . . . *a Villager*, etc.) which chronicle life in a fictitious rural community – at least I think it's fictitious! He too is sure that the Christmas of today has changed greatly from the way it used to be in West Country:

I think that the most striking difference now, as opposed to up to about the First World War, is how rich we are [Aunt Mabel had also mentioned money] because in the old days I suppose that the average peasant in the West Country was little better off than the peasants living in the Third World today, which is very close to the starvation line. But it was the one time of the year when everybody made a huge effort to have a real feast. Of course Christmas fell in mid-winter when food was short anyway and so the Christmas dinner and the Christmas celebration was an enormously important event and thought about for the whole year. We've lost a lot of that. You probably had to go to church twice a day, did

Aunt Mabel Mudge of The Drewe Arms,
Drewsteignton

113

your carol singing and looked enviously at the squire, who was probably warm in a coat when you had none at all, but it was mainly that Christmas was so much more important then than it is now. Not for spiritual reasons, but a matter of keeping body and soul together, or rather body together. I would have hated to have lived then. You made a present out of something that you found in the fields as a toy for your child because you couldn't afford to buy one. Only the man at the top, the squire, could celebrate Christmas in any sort of way that we could understand now.

Bob Cann, who is retired now and lives in South Tawton, was awarded the CBE in the Queen's New Year's honours list in 1989 for his services to folk music as a master on the accordion and a great story-teller. He also remembers how different things used to be:

We used to hang up a little stocking and all you'd get back then was a packet of sweets and a couple of oranges. You didn't get no toys like you get today. You'd wake up in the morning and there would be your stocking, and sometimes Mother had made a trip into the city and to Woolworths, and you would get a little imitation stocking with a few humbugs in or things like that and we thought that this was wonderful, as kids.

Aunt Mabel remembers Christmas as a very happy time: 'Very jolly it was. Father Christmas used to come to the village school.' This event is also recalled by Jack Price from when he was a lad in Drewsteignton:

We had our evening's entertainment when we had to sing and dance and perform, and then the highlight of the evening would come with the arrival of Father Christmas.

# · A West Country Christmas ·

We had to stand around the Christmas tree in a circle, and sing a carol. My memory is that we were moving around the tree in a circle, knowing full well that Father Christmas would come in that door over in the corner. We would all be watching the door as we walked around singing our carol. Everybody's eyes would be on that door and then, suddenly, Father Christmas would arrive! He was all jolly and laughing and everything would come to a halt. Father Christmas would be welcomed by the Headmaster, who of course (I know since) would know him very well, and they'd have a bit of backchat about what sort of journey he'd had and where he'd parked his reindeer and we'd all be listening to this. It was a moment of pure magic.

Then we would stand still for a moment, while the presents were distributed. Members of staff would climb up on step-ladders and snip off the presents, which would all be named, from the tree. Our names would be read out and we'd walk proudly forward to pick up our presents from Father Christmas no less! Well, of course, Father Christmas, being a village man, knew each one of us very well and he'd have a special word to say to each child as he gave them their present. 'How's your finger now? Is it better?' We would gasp at this and think, 'Father Christmas knows about my bad finger. Isn't that absolutely marvellous?' 'And you, little Jimmy, did you find that football the other evening? The one that you lost down by the hedge?' Jimmy's mouth would fall open in wonder at Father Christmas knowing about his football that he lost the other night. 'What a man he is!'

And so all the presents would be distributed and then there would be three cheers for Father Christmas and he'd wave us goodbye and wish us a Merry Christmas, and then he'd be through the door and gone. A bell would tinkle in the background and we were still wrapped up and lost in those moments of pure magic.

# · A West Country Christmas ·

There's a lady called Martha, who, along with her husband Ned, lives at Whiddon Down. Does she look forward to Christmas as much as those schoolchildren obviously did?

Well, I do and I don't. Us don't really like Christmas. Something always goes wrong in our house when 'tis Christmas. It has done ever since we've had the children small, you know. One Christmas I remember I said, 'Put the turkey in the oven.' Us done our work, then went to church, and then come home and had our dinner. Then I helped out with the Christmas pudding. Well, there us was sitting around in the kitchen, eating our Christmas pudding, and enjoying it because it was a beautiful recipe of my old mother's, and suddenly one of the boys started to cry. I said to Father, 'There's something wrong with that boy.' I said, 'Look at him. Get over and pat him on the back.' So Father went over and give the boy a good pat on the back and the boy went a bit purple and spluttered and managed to tell us that he'd swallowed his sixpence!

Then I remember another year, when things didn't seem too bad and I thought, 'Now this is better, this is going alright, this is.' Us had got through the day pretty well. Us had had tea, and then us went in front room, you do that Christmas night don't ye? You light the fire and it smokes all day – it don't burn right until it's time to go to bed – but you sit there with your eyes watering and stick it out when all of a sudden one of the boys started to cry again. I thought, 'There you are! I thought that it was going too good to be true.' The boy kept pointing to his ear so I said to Father, 'Get on and have a look in the boy's ear.' Well, he lit a candle and nearly set fire to the boy! I said, 'Why don't you go in the kitchen and get the flashlight?' So he come in with the flashlight and looked in the boy's ear. 'Cor Mother,' he said, 'you'll never guess what I've seed. You

# · *A West Country Christmas* ·

Ned and Martha 'Annaford, alias June Smith and Edna
Dunning

want to look in the little boy's ear.' So I did. I took the torch out of his hand and looked in the boy's ear and, to tell you the truth, I nearly passed out. Do you know when I looked in that boy's ear, there was an eye looking at me. It was only the eye off his teddy bear, but you have a glass of sherry at Christmas time and look in somebody's ear and see an eye! It don't half give you a turn!

Just two of the Christmas stories from Martha, alias June Smith, who, with Edna Dunning as Ned, are well-known entertainers throughout the West Country.

Martha mentioned turkey, which is of course very much the

centre piece of the Christmas Day meal today, but it wasn't always that way, as Bob Cann told me:

Christmas Day, you'd have a jolly good feed. All the farm workers and quarry men, nearly every one of them, kept a pig, poultry and ducks back in those days. Mother used to have right across our kitchen, hanging from the beams, sides of pig, shoulders and bacon, and at Christmas this huge ham would be brought down and cooked for the whole family. We nearly always used to have a goose as well. That was self reared of course. We very seldom had a turkey – you just couldn't afford it; it was only the gentry that had turkey then. The working class never bothered to rear turkey: they were a delicate thing to rear, so it was goose or duck. Although we were poor, there was always loads to eat and plenty of cider.

What about the excitement, that magic that Jack Price spoke of? Bob Cann says:

It couldn't come quick enough really when we was kids. It seemed endless waiting for Father Christmas as a little kid. At Christmas time, usually on Christmas Eve, the whole family would get together and we'd have the old concertinas going. There'd be dancing and then bed, but you'd have a job to go to sleep waiting for Father Christmas to come. You'd wake up in the morning and there at the end of the bed would be your stocking and a little present, and the bottle of beer that we'd left for Father Christmas would have been drunk. It's funny that, he never left any beer behind. In fact, my father, who used to keep a lot of cider, would put out a bottle of cider for him as well and that too would be gone in the morning!

Jack Price can remember helping his father put out

something for Father Christmas as well:

> When he'd arrive, he would be hungry and thirsty so I'd help prepare a place for him. We put out a bottle of beer, a glass and a plate of bread and cheese. We'd also put out some oats, which my father got from a neighbouring farmer, for the reindeer. Then it was off to bed to try and get some sleep so as to wake early in the morning, and the excitement of the presents and unpacking them sitting up in bed. Then my mother would call me, 'Jack, Jack, Father Christmas has been!' I would rush downstairs to find that the beer had been drunk, the bread and cheese more or less cleared and there would be soot marks and sooty finger prints on the table cloth where Father Christmas had had his supper before leaving and going on his rounds.

Tony Beard, who is a well known West Country broadcaster and entertainer – perhaps better known as 'The Wag from Widecombe' – has some particular memories of a country Christmas as well:

> I remember my grandmother and grandfather used to always hang up their stockings and, invariably, when my cousin and I went down to see them on Christmas Day, one of us had my grandmother's stocking and the other had grandpa's stocking, and there was always the old fashioned things that you found in a Christmas stocking. There was an orange – nowadays oranges are here all the year round but years ago oranges used to arrive at Christmas time – there was a lump of coal, a handful of nuts and a few sweets and, do you know, we treasured that. That was really the highlight of Christmas.
>
> I think that it's rather a pity now that everything that you see in the press or on television, some game or some toy, it's only £39.99. Only! That's what I think is the

Tony Beard

vexing part, it makes children think, 'Oh it's only that. We can have that,' and, 'Oh it's only that, so we can have that as well,' but when we were kids it wasn't like that. I can remember in the war that there was a gentleman in the parish who made a toy for every child at Christmas. There was a village Christmas tree and Father Christmas would arrive at the tree and present us all with a toy that this man had made. He made me a tank out of wood. It took a masterful hammering. It was knocked about, rolled over, thrown about, and it survived. But the tragedy now is that with a lot of the presents that you buy for children they hardly survive unwrapping, leave alone the end of the day. But that stuff that we had then, it survived for years.

Just because it was Christmas in the country, it didn't mean that the work could come to a halt, as Bob Cann and Charlie Hill, both of whom grew up on farms, told me:

You all had your little chores to do. It was all open fires back then so you had to go out, help carry in sticks and feed the poultry. It was a fairly busy day for us kids. Your life on the farm carried on much the same as any other working day. All the hay had to be got in, because it wasn't in bales, and all the root crops had to be got in for the bullocks. And a week before Christmas mother would have all the Christmas poultry to get ready and you'd be helping her with the plucking and the delivering.

Betty Johns from Payhembury can remember the poultry-plucking vividly: 'There was no electric, so it all had to be done by hand, and we often used to do it round the open fire in the kitchen. It was mostly chickens that we were plucking and ducks and geese and the feathers would be collected in baths.'

Tony Beard, as well as being a broadcaster and entertainer, is also a farmer:

One thing that I always enjoy on Christmas Day is the afternoon work. The fact is that you have just got to get up from Christmas dinner and get out on the farm for an hour or so in the afternoon and go round and see the bullocks and the cows, and I think that that is the best cure for indigestion that you can possibly have. It doesn't matter how much you've had to eat for Christmas Day dinner, you've got to go out – and there's something really lovely about it. Plenty of fresh air, it's just like ordinary people going out for an hour's stroll, but for us it's a question of having to go out and do your work. That's one of the highlights of Christmas Day for me, and then you can come back and start eating all over again!

As I noted earlier, farmers aren't the only ones who have to work at Christmas time, a fact that didn't escape Jack Price's notice either:

Christmas Day didn't make much difference to my parents, who for years ran the Post Office on the village square in Drewsteignton. They had to be up at their normal time of half-past five because there was a delivery on Christmas Day and they had to be ready to receive the mail van. Many people timed posting their presents and their letters to arrive and be delivered on Christmas Day. I used to awake at an early hour to all the excitement that was going on in the sorting office. There'd be postmen with paper hats on, singing as they were sorting the mail, and there'd be a drink, and then all the postmen would go out on their deliveries. My father, as well as being post-master was also a postman and he was always back in good time from his fourteen-mile delivery round to wash and change, ready for our family Christmas dinner.

# · A West Country Christmas ·

Christmas fare in Ilfracombe High Street at the turn of
the century

My parents-in-law told me stories about their local postman
who used to linger on their farm for a drink on Christmas Day
and set off again a little more uncertainly on his bike for more
hospitality at the next farm. Tony Beard, too, had a tale about
a postman, 'a smashing chap', named Sid Bray:

> He was a real character and I think he was one of the
> postmen that was really sorry when Christmas Day
> deliveries stopped. He was a lovely chap and, irrespective of
> whether it was raining buckets or snowing, he would always
> greet my mother with, 'Hello Missus, 'tis a lovely day.'
> Coming up to Christmas itself, of course, all us kids used to
> write our letters to Father Christmas, and Sid would take
> them from us and see that they got to Father Christmas and
> were dealt with in the proper manner. What made his
> Christmas was, on Christmas Day, all us kids coming
> we had got. He used to get three sheets to the wind, of

course, come the end of Christmas Day, because everybody loved him and everybody had a drink for Sid. He was one of the real characters, the sort that have disappeared with the modern Christmas. Most of the postmen, of course, must have been thrilled to bits when they didn't have to deliver on Christmas Day, particularly the family men; but Sid was a bachelor and he got his Christmas cheer from seeing all the kids with their presents.

Christmas Day itself wasn't always given over totally to enjoyment. Bob Cann told me that they never, as a family, played cards on Christmas Day, and if they did play games, it was never for money, only peas or beans. So, for many, although it was a celebration, it was to be strictly observed.

However kept, there is no doubt that Christmas in the West Country, as elsewhere, is and was a family time, although Martha (June Smith, of course) has her doubts as to whether it's a good idea to invite relatives to stay:

Don't talk to me about relatives! I shall never forget last Christmas, never as long as I live. I asked Granny to stay. He can't stand the sight of my mother, but I wasn't going to take no notice of he so I wrote and asked Granny if her'd like to come for Christmas and Granny said her would. Well, he went up the village on Christmas Eve and met Granny off the bus with the pony and trap, and I put her to bed with a nice hot cup of cocoa. Then I said to Father, 'I think that I'll go to bed myself,' because Christmas, you know, is a busy old time.

I got half-way up the stairs and I realised I hadn't iced me cake. I'd made him like you should. Had him in a tin for about six weeks, I had, but I hadn't had time to ice him. So I come down and I said to Father, 'I can't have Granny sitting up to Christmas tea and no icing on the cake.' So, although I was tired, I got a basin, made a bit of icing and put it on top of the old cake. And then I said to Father – 'Oh what a pity! I haven't got nothing to put on him.' Well, he's got a push bike, so he said, 'Hang on a bit, Mother,' and he went out in the shed and he come in with a little old baccy tin with a few ball-bearings in him. So I washed them off and polished them up and put them around the edge of the cake, and, although I say so myself, the old cake didn't look bad. Then he had a brain-wave. He went behind the picture and broke off a bit of holly and us stuck it in the middle, and, although I say so meself, the cake looked handsome.

I went to bed happy that night. The turkey was in the dairy, all stuffed, Granny was tucked up in bed asleep, and the cake was all iced. Oh, I went to bed and slept well, I did. Well, us got up in the morning, did our work, went to church and had our dinner, and listened to the Queen. He went out and milked the cows, and then it was tea-time.

I know that you should start with a bit of bread and butter, but granny asked for a bit of cake. I said to Father, 'Give her a nice big bit, there's plenty there,' so he did. He cut her a nice big bit of cake and her sat down and eat it and enjoyed it. Then darn me, if she didn't ask for another bit! I said to Father, 'Get on and give her another bit, plenty there,' so he did. He cut her another nice big bit of cake but us forgot to tell her about the balls. But it didn't seem to make no difference, because her eats without her teeth in, and her wobbled it about a bit and got it down alright. Well, then us went into the front room – we all do it every year don't we? Go into the front room and sit beside the fire and have a little glass of what you fancy, whether 'tis sherry or whether 'tis whisky or whether 'tis a little drop of made a wish, he would go off down to the room at the other home-made wine or a glass of cider. Then you have a fig, then you'll have a date, then you'll have a nut or two, then perhaps you have another drop of sherry, then you'll have an orange and then there's that old box of Turkish delight – 'tis eating all the time isn't it? Well, that was when disaster struck. Granny got up, went to poke the fire, passed wind and shot the cat!

June Smith put the character of Martha to one side during the programme, as she gave me some of her own thoughts on Christmas:

Do you know, I think that the children today miss so much. They think that they've got such a lot, but on the other hand they've got so little because it doesn't seem to matter how much they have, they're never content. You never went shopping like you do today and there were no catalogues. The children today get out a catalogue and they say, I want this, I want that. In my day there was no such thing as 'I want', you just had to wait and see what you got, and everything that you got, whether it was little or large, was absolute magic. You had so little and you were grateful as a child for everything that you had.

Another memory of mine is the preparation of the Christmas puddings. We were a large family and it wasn't just a question of making one pudding: my mother would make eight or nine puddings and it would take two days to prepare them. The fruit would come in bags from the grocer, all weighed out. It wouldn't be pre-washed as it is today, so my mother would sit to the table with a bowl of hot water and she would get the stones out from the dried raisins and wash her fingers off every so often in the bowl of water, because they were so sticky. So had the raisins to be prepared. The candied peel would come in great, big strips

A joint of beef for the Christmas table: Ilfracombe butchers
in 1894

and that had to be chopped. Today you get it in a carton, all
chopped, but not then. My mother would sit to the table
and chop this candied peel, and to pinch a little bit and
taste it was lovely! The cherries would be washed and
quartered and breadcrumbs would be made and the
butcher's suet would have to be chopped very finely. So that
would take a day, the preparation of all these goodies. Oh
the smell of the spices, the lemon rind and the orange peel!
Then the next day, my mother and elder sister would mix it
all in a great, big bowl. Then my father would come, and
he'd be the first to stir it after the eggs and the brandy had
been added. Mother would go to the cutlery basket and get
out a large silver spoon and Dad would give the first stir. He
always used that same spoon and would make such a
ceremony out of it. Then, whilst the rest of us had a stir and

end of the house where he had his desk and come back with a handful of sixpences.

The coins would be washed in hot water, and then they would be added to the mixture in the big bowl and stirred in. It would be a real surprise if you were the one to get a sixpence. The next day, the copper would be lit – the old-fashioned wash boiler – and all these puddings would be put in, in their basins, tied around with a bit of cloth, and they would be boiled for about eight hours. The fire would be kept going all day and the puddings would be going glug, glug, glug, and then they would be stored away and on Christmas Day the biggest one would be brought out, and put on to boil again that morning. When it was served, if you had one of those sixpences, that was real luck!

Of course, back in those days there was no radio or television, and you had to provide your own entertainment. Music was a very important part of Christmas to a lot of people, along with dancing, as Bob Cann told me:

Back then the men didn't wear shoes or nothing like that, it was nail boots, and at Christmas time and on Sundays, of course, they got out their best boots and many families would push back the table and start step dancing. They would dance on the granite floor, and with the music and the rattle of the boots, it was great!

It must have been, and a far cry from the way in which we celebrate Christmas today. You might have felt the cold more (you couldn't just turn up the central heating then), and perhaps you had to make do with a token present of whatever came to hand, but Christmas seems to have been marked in a more memorable way and, in spite of what James Robertson says, I know which way of celebrating I prefer. Happy Christmas!

# A West Country Dialect Christmas

## EVE CLIST

*Now here's a treat for you, as Eve Clist from Hemyock, on the Devon/Somerset border, recalls 'A West Country Dialect Christmas'. It perhaps misses something without her glorious accent, but I hope that you will get the general drift.*

I ain't for saying how old I be, but yer I might s'well tell 'ee, I be eighty-four. Eighty-four years young now, so when was that? Nineteen-hundred-and-four, I reckon I was born bout 'e then. Well, give or tek a year or two you know, it don't make much difference do it? Not one year or two, I don't think so anyway. Sometimes I says I be eighty-one and sometimes I says I be eighty-nine, but that don't matter.

The first Christmas that I can remember was when my father was in the army because he was a regular soldier, zee. He was a Sergeant Major. He said 'twas better for him to be a Sergeant Major that 'twas vor en to be a Captain, you see 'e'd have to live it up if 'e was Captain. Nineteen-hundred-and-ten was the first Christmas that I can mind us having all sorts of things. Mind you, us didn't get a lot I can tell 'ee, us didn't get a lot. But a week or two before Christmas when us was saying our prayers, Mother would say, 'You must ask God for a pram, a doll and tea-set and a piano.' So I got all that off, so. Course, us didn't know whether us was going to get it or no, but sure enough when Christmas morning come there was a pram, a little wooden affair with two or dree wheels and you could push en along, a ramshackly 'fair 'twas, and the tea-set was one of those yer tiny ones (Cor! I wish I'd got en now, he'd be worth a fortune, but I ain't got en now so that's that) and the piano. 'E'd got about fourteen notes, this y piano and I could play 'God Save the Queen' and my brother Bill, he could play it. 'E played by his yer see, 'e didn't knaw no music. I knawed music, but 'e, Bill, didn't, so he played with his haid and I played by the music.

The thought of it makes me proper nostalgic. I can also remember when Old Clammer Boot Jarman used to call for Mother's Christmas order. Her used to zend us kids upstairs, because her said that little people had big yers and eyes – but her didn't know what we was up to. You zee, there was a crack in they vlorboard, upstairs, right 'cross the room, so us all gor down on all fours peeping down and us could zee everything, and yer most of it, and us would tick off on our own list all us yerd, and what one didn'yer, t'other did.

There was the time when Bill valled down the stairs when he was carring up our tea; he broke all our lovely mugs and scalded his veet and so had to 'ave they bandaged up all through Christmas.

Arter Father left the army, us didn't keep up Christmas Day, because he had to go to work. He was a postman. Me and Bill used to go round with Father and help him round with his mail, and minds coming down Station Road one wet Christmas morning and letting all the letters fall abroad and us had to scrabble em up and there us was trying to find out whose was whose. I reckon that us made a few mistakes that morning. We never heard nort 'bout it arterwards, but I reckon us did.

# · *A West Country Christmas* ·

Us didn't have a bad dinner come Christmas Day. Mother might have got an old hen that was on its last legs like, but 'er used to tenderize un a bit see. Well, I don't know what 'er done to un but 'twas never very tender, I can tell ee, but us had got good grinders, I can tell 'ee.

And then, in the arternoon, Mother would have us in the front room and ur'd have a gurt big bag beside o'er. Us knawed what was in the bag though us 'tended us didn't. 'Can us have some monkey-nuts, Mother?' us'd ask her. And 'er'd gee us some of they ther old monkey-nuts and us'd vly en at each other and have a fine bit of fun. And then old Dad would come in and he always had to read us a bit of Dickens. 'E always used to read about the Old Scrooge. We always had to have that un every year. We were so pleased when Old Scrooge turned out to be a decent, good, kind-hearted fellow arter all.

I can remember that Ralph was terribly keen on that Mecarno and they used to make a model and once they made an airplane and they flied un 'cross the room, from one side to t'other. That was wonderful to see that thing flying.

Oh aye, I must mind to tell ye this too. The folks down below see they's come up to us on Christmas Day. They'd come in and sit down. We didn't know 'em very well and we didn't see why they should come and eat our good food 'cos we didn't have so much as they did anyway. But, anyway, we made them as welcome as us could, and any rate they'd bide there a bit and then someone would say, 'Us'll sing a few carols.' Us always started with 'Christians Awake!' – I don't knaw why, 'cos it was in the middle of the afternoon, but us'd always start with that. I tell ye, us had some fun back in they days us did.

# Chris'mas Invitation

## WILLIAM BARNES

*This third poem by William Barnes is from a collection
called* Poems in Dorset Dialect, *published in 1844.*

Come down to-morow night; an' mind
Don't leave thy fiddle-bag behind;
We'll sheake a lag, an' drink a cup
O'eale, to keep wold Chris'mas up.

An' let thy sister teake thy earm,
The walk won't do her any harm;
There's noo dirt now to spweil her frock,
The ground's a-vroze so hard's a rock.

You won't meet any stranger's feace,
But only neighbours o'the pleace,
An 'Stowe, an' Combe; an' two or dree
Vrom uncle's up at Rookery.

An' thou wu'lt vind a rwosy feace,
An' peair ov eyes so black as sloos,
The prettiest woones in all the pleace, –
I'm sure I needen tell thee whose.

We got a back-bran, dree girt logs
So much as dree ov us can car;

# · A West Country Christmas ·

We'll put 'em up athirt the dogs,
An' meake a vier to the bar.

An' ev'ry woone shall tell his teale,
An' ev'ry woone shall zing his zong,
An' ev'ry woone wull drink his eale
To love an' frien'ship all night long.

We'll snap the tongs, we'll have a ball,
We'll shake the house, we'll lift the ruf,
We'll romp an' meake the maidens squall,
A'catchen o'm at blind-man's buff.

Zoo come to-morrow night; an' mind,
Don't leave thy fiddle-bag behind;
We'll shake a lag, an' drink a cup
O'eale, to keep wold Chris'mas up.

The snow-covered West Country from the air, 1987

133

# A Merry Christmas to all our Readers

*This is a phrase we are quite used to seeing at the end of the year in newspapers, magazines and periodicals, as the editors and staff wish their readership a Merry Christmas and the compliments of the season. Here's how it was done in 1781 by the predecessors of the present-day news-vendors in Sherborne, Dorset.*

THE NEW-YEAR'S GIFT of the MEN who distribute THE SHERBORNE JOURNAL To Their worthy MASTERS and MISTRESSES on the Entrance of the New Year

> Masters, around your Christmas Fire,
> I hope your honours sit at ease;
> Come and draw your chairs a little nigher,
> And take my Madams on your knees;
> Then you shall hear, in language plain;
> Your trusty newsman's annual strain:
> For 'tis my duty, and my pride,
> To greet you, every New-Year's-Tide.
>
> Ah, would that, in these homely rhymes,
> I could foretell you better times;
> Or fill my verse with other things
> Than tales of Ministers and Kings,
> At the whole command, from shore to shore,
> We hear the thundering cannon roar,

And see, on many a bloody plain,
In heaps the wounded and the slain –
Well, Heaven be praised, my worthy Masters,
That We are safe from these disasters;
And far from gun-powder and steel,
Need only hear what others feel.

I never lik'd, upon my word,
Either the musquet, or the sword;
Trumpets and drums are fine, 'tis true;
And what can beat a grand review?
'Tis a brave fight, I needs must say,
When all march out, in bold array,
And, without making one rank thinner,
March home again, and go to dinner:
But when you come to warlike blows,
No quiet man can relish those;
What? – cut and slash? – I'll go no further –
'Tis murther, Masters, downright murther!

Peace then, your Honours, Peace, you see,
Is, sure enough, the thing for Me:
And if I guess the matter right,
'Tis what would give us all delight –
Ah, with what pleasure should I trudge it,
If such good news were in my budget!
Instead of that, oh, bless my stars,
'Tis nothing else but Wars, Wars, Wars!

Across the seas, a great way over,
Farther by half than 'tis to Dover,
We first begun, I hear folks say,
A very foolish, wicked fray;
And, making sure to rule the roost,
Abused the friends that loved us most.

Now, Masters, I could never see,
How this with wisdom did agree;
Nor could I, for my soul, approve
All that was ordered, up above;
And sooth to say, I always found
Much discontent throughout my Round –
Next, as your Honours know full well,
The French and Spaniards came pell-mell,
Making as if they'd eat us all;
Howe'er, their pride soon got a fall.
And now I hear the plodding Dutch
Shew a month's mind to have a touch:
Well, well, Mynheers, few words are best,
We'll put your metal to the test;
And shew you too, or soon or later,
How 'tis to fish in troubled water.

But hold! – I must not go too far –
We have not yet a new Dutch war;
And who can say if second thoughts
May not correct all present faults?
Then let that pass, just as it may,
And wonder that a Newsman's tongue
Should run so freely, and so long.

Ah, worthy Masters, let me tell ye,
Rhyming depends upon the belly.
Pudding and beef, and such like diet,
Soon make the greatest rhymesters quiet:
Then if you wish to have me gone,
Speak but the word, the thing is done;
Put me within the pantry door,
I'll warrant you shall hear no more.

# A Christmas Selection from the Newspapers

## GEORGE PRIDMORE

*George Pridmore is a writer and broadcaster, who is to be heard regularly on BBC Local Radio in the south-west. He is also a newspaper historian and has a unique and very extensive collection of local, national and international newspapers dating back to 1673. From that collection, George has put together this review of how the papers reported just some of the West Country Christmases of years gone by.*

**Christmas Giving and Taking – from the *Bath Chronicle*, 1822**

On Christmas Eve, the Rev W.H.H. Hartley distributed at Bucklebury House his annual donation of 16 fat sheep, and a proportionate quantity of bread, among the poor of his parish.

\* \* \*

Mr Parish, with his accustomed benevolence, ordered the inmates of the Penitentiary, on Christmas Day, a plentiful

dinner of roast beef, plum pudding and strong beer; a like dinner to the paupers in Bathwick poor-house, and a plenteous feast to the prisoners in the city gaol.

\* \* \*

The landlords of the Bush and White Inns, in Bristol, kept 'open houses' on Christmas Day, and many a hungry and thirsty soul partook of their bounty.

\* \* \*

John Merris Esq of Salisbury, ordered six fat sheep to be distributed among 65 poor families in his neighbourhood.

\* \* \*

V. Stuckley Esq, High Sheriff for his county [Dorset], ordered a liberal distribution to the poor of Langport.

\* \* \*

George Coombs and William Clark were committed on Monday to Devizes Bridewell by T.H. Phipp Esq, for stealing 21 ducks and 4 drakes from Longbridge-Deverell on Christmas Eve; they were stopped by the Bath officers on Christmas Day, while offering them for sale.

## Lyme Regis Christmas Landslip of 1839

Christmas Day of 1839 was one which farm labourer William Critchard and his family from Lyme Regis on the Dorset/Devon border would have undoubtedly remembered for the rest of their lives.

William Critchard was employed by Mr Chappell at Bindon Farm, and he and the Critchard family occupied one of a number of cottages on the Dowlands undercliff between the towns of Lyme Regis and Seaton. On 23 December, having found it difficult to shut his front door, he noticed that cracks had started to appear in the plastering of the walls of his cottage. The next evening, Christmas Eve, William and his wife, left their children in bed while they made their way to Bindon Farm, along with other farm labourers, to join in some seasonal merrymaking, which included the burning of the ashen faggot. It was about one o'clock in the morning as they were making their way back home that Christmas Day when they discovered much to their alarm that the pathway down the cliff to their cottage had sunk by a foot.

They retired to bed, but were awakened at about five in the morning by the sound of the cottage literally cracking apart. William opened the front door with great difficulty and saw large cracks in the ground surrounding the cottage. Having warned the occupiers of other cottages and removing his household valuables, William set off to Bindon Farm to tell his employer. The path had now sunk a further six feet!

During Christmas Day, as the land began to move further, the other farm labourers evacuated their cottages and shifted their belongings to safety. The climax came that night – with a terrific noise and the effect of an earthquake, a whole area of land slipped into the sea and the Critchards' home disappeared completely, while other cottages were left in ruins.

One hundred years later, in a special commemorative article published by *Pulman's Weekly News* in 1939, the happenings on that fateful Christmas Day of 1839 were described as 'one of the most remarkable phenomena ever recorded', and the paper went on to describe how 'the remarkable scene was visited by Queen Victoria and many scientists', and how 'sightseers in their thousands flocked there and innumerable thousands more have visited it during the past one hundred years'. As I said at the beginning, that Christmas must have been one that William Critchard and his family would have remembered for a long, long time.

# · *A West Country Christmas* ·

**A Victorian Christmas – extracts from the** *Western Daily Mercury*, **1871**

*23 December. Christmas 1871.* Yesterday the Right Worshipful Mayor of Devonport (J. May Esq) with his usual liberality, presented the whole of the police force the handsome sum of six shillings and eight pence each as a Christmas present.

*24 December. Christmas! Christmas!! Christmas!!! – The Mystery Disclosed.* With what astonishment have ladies received the intelligence, on asking their friends as a great favour, their receipts for making such beautiful light Pie-crusts, Puddings, Cakes, Fancy Bread etc., to find the secret rested entirely on using WOOD'S Baking Powder! See you get Wood's as none other will answer. Sold in packets at 1d. and 2d. each, also in cannisters at 1s. each, by all grocers. Also by the proprietor W. Woods, Chemist, Bedford Street, Plymouth.

*26 December. Christmas Day at the Newton Union.* The whole of the paupers in this Union were provided with such a sumptuous dinner of roast beef and plum pudding so as to convince them that, although isolated from the world, they were not forgotten by those who were enjoying themselves in more favourable circumstances. The attention and kindness they received from the master (Mr Moxey) were all that could be desired.

*27 December. Christmas Festivities at Par.* A Christmas Tree was erected yesterday in the Wesleyan school-room. It was embellished with useful and ornamental articles, the proceeds of the sale of which are to be applied to the liquidation of the debt on the chapel, belonging to the place. A public tea was provided, and the tree was soon denuded of all extraneous matter.

*28 December. Amusements.* Theatre Royal, Plymouth. Every Evening during the week a grand comic CHRISTMAS

PANTOMIME based on Planche's Burlesque and arranged for this establishment by Mr E.W. Royce. Entitled THE YELLOW DWARF or HARLEQUIN KING OF THE GOLD MINES AND THE QUEEN OF THE FAIRY BLONDES. The scenery and Grand Transformation by Mr Chas Wood. Box plan now open at Mr Sawday's Music Warehouse, 15 and 16 George Street, where places for the Orchestra and Dress Balcony Stalls may be secured.

*29 December. Torquay Christmas Ball.* The Annual Christmas Ball was held at the Bath Saloon, Torquay, on Wednesday evening and was numerously attended. The dancing took place in the large room, the other being used for a refreshment room. The refreshments were supplied by Mr Rolph of the Victoria Parade. The arrangements were satisfactorily carried out by Mr G.M. Tripe, the manager. Mr Round's Subscription Band was in attendance and played an excellent selection of music.

## A Gruesome Christmas Awakening of 1875

There could hardly be any more gruesome way of starting Christmas Day than to be awakened and told that you have been sleeping with a corpse! That is what happened to a lady named Mary Edwards at Bristol on Christmas Day in 1875, according to a report in the following week's edition of the *West Somerset Free Press*. Under the heading, 'Sad Termination to a Christmas Party', the paper described how a Mrs Mary Gillard of Draycott was staying with her son Francis at Morley Street, Bristol, for Christmas. After spending the evening with the family, she 'retired to rest' in the early hours of Christmas Day with her friend Mary Edwards. The report went on to say that about a couple of hours later Francis Gillard had occasion to go into the bedroom and was shocked

With Good and Seasonable Wishes.

to find his parent dead. The *West Somerset Free Press* concluded: 'She had expired so quietly that the person sleeping with her was not aware that anything had happened and was slumbering peacefully by the side of a corpse.'

## A Boer War Christmas, 1899

Christmas of 1899 was overshadowed by the Boer War, which had started a couple of months earlier. This was emphasised by the editorial of the *Devon Weekly Times* of 22 December, which began: 'Once more Christmas is now at hand and following time-honoured custom we should wish our readers the Compliments of the Season. But we feel it is almost a mockery to bid our constant "A Merry Christmas". Individual sorrows and bereavements come to us all in turn and are present at Christmas as well as at other periods of the year. But the days of this December are nationally dark. At a season when our ministers should preach "Peace and Goodwill", we are engaged in most sanguinary warfare.'

However, despite the somewhat gloomy tones of its editorial, the advertisement columns of that same issue of the *Devon Weekly Times* offered its readers the opportunity to engage in the customary Christmas feasting and festivities. For example, one such advertisement read:

### CHRISTMAS SPECIALITIES
(Selections from our list)

| Muscatels | 8d./10d./1s. | Crystallised Fruits | from 5d. per box. |
|---|---|---|---|
| Jordan almonds | 2d. | Bon-bons | from 5d. per box. |
| French plums | 6d. | Fancy tin biscuits | from 5d. per box. |
| Prunes | 5d. | Oranges – 20, 30 and 40 | 1s. |
| Apple rings | 6d. | Hams – the finest | 7½d. |
| Apricots | 8d. | Picnic hams – the finest | 4½d. |
| Pears | 9d. | Bath chaps – | |
| Iced cakes | 6d. | smoked. | 6d. |

Dulcemona Tea in glove boxes, 1s. 6d. and 1s. 10d. (Useful present.) We propose GIVING AWAY during Christmas one of our MAGNIFICENT ALMANACKS to every purchase of 2s. upwards.

JOHN BARNES, The Stores, Paul Street
THE PEOPLE'S SUPPLY STORES, EXETER

# · A West Country Christmas ·

## A Working Christmas – extracts from the *Western Times*, 26 December 1916

Christmas work at Exeter Post Ofice: Generally speaking the volume of work dealt with at Exeter Post Office compared favourably with last year. At the Head Office in the High Street, the staff is very largely composed of female clerks and they were able to cope with the pressure satisfactorily. The staff were augmented by the employment of women both in the sorting and postmen's departments. The way in which the women faced the inclement weather during the past fortnight was a demonstration of the earnestness with which the gentler sex are determined to do their part in the great crisis.

Christmas passed quietly in Exeter. Gladness was brought to a number of households by the presence of soldier members of the family on home service who were among the fortunate ten per cent released for Christmas leave, and in a few other instances, by men back from the front for a few days' respite from the rigours and anxieties of trench warfare. Their home-coming naturally was most welcome at such a time, and the cheery optimism which they brought with them, did a deal towards giving hope and confidence to friends at home as to the outcome of the struggle.

## Christmas Earthquake, 1923 – something went bump in the night!

The usual seasonal festivities of several South Devon folk on the evening of Christmas Day in 1923 were rudely interrupted by a very strange happening. It was something in the form of a distinct tremor, which caused houses to shake, set crockery vibrating on shelves and in cupboards, started windows rattling, and alarmed poultry and farm livestock. 'Earthquake Shock' and 'A Remarkable Experience in South Devon' were the headlines above a report of the incident in the *Western Times* on 28 December, which began:

> Apparently South Devon experienced a slight shock of earthquake on Christmas night over a wide area . . . Parents thought that their children had fallen out of bed and went upstairs to investigate, while others who happened to be upstairs, considering there were strange noises below, made an examination of the rooms.

The tremor was noticed at South Brent, Rattery, Diptford, Harberton, Harberton Ford and Totnes. One lady told the *Western Times*: 'We thought it was heavy thunder, but it was something different. The floor shook with a funny vibration as if there was something underneath it.' Another described it as 'a sound like heavy furniture being drawn about a room and then falling over'.

**Shopping Specials – from** *Cornish Evening Tidings*, 1933

In the 1930s, the delightfully named *Cornish Evening Tidings* – the daily edition of the *Cornishman*, and published on Mondays, Tuesdays, Thursdays, Fridays and Saturdays – used to issue what it called 'Christmas Shopping Special Editions'.

'Shop now – Only 7 shopping days to Xmas' the paper reminded its readers in such an edition on Friday 15 December 1933. That reminder appeared in the top corner of a front page made up of three large advertisements. One of these listed a number of 'Gifts that Please', available at Radborne's, 111a, Market Jew Street; another invited readers to 'Come and Select your Christmas gifts from the New Open Store' – Knees, The Terrace, and Wood Street, Penzance; while a third reminded ladies that, 'for Xmas Parties and Dances you must look your best', an invitation to call at 'The Parisian Hairdressing Coy.', Causeway, Penzance.

An advertisement on an inside page of this same edition assured readers, 'You are sure to find your boy's present at Turner's'. On offer were:

'Wickets' – The Game of Genuine Skill
'P.M.' – The Game for Everyone
Real Telephones for the home
Hornby Trains, Meccano and Steam Engines
Chemistry and electrical sets
Miniature Billards Table

And if the reader was in any doubt, Turner's advertisement advised him or her that, 'Corinthian Bagatelle is still the rage'.

### 'Christmas Jokes'

Christmas is of course a time to make merry and a time for jokes and this column of that 1933 issue of the *Cornish Evening Tidings* contained such seasonal gems as:

VICAR      You are not in our Christmas coal club this year, Thomas?

THOMAS      No sir, the missus and me didn't think it wur necessary. Us do live next door to the coal yard now!'

\* \* \*

Before the fire on Christmas Eve two youngish ladies were chatting. 'Mollie', said the prettier of the two, 'would a stocking hold all you would like for Christmas?'

'No,' said the other, 'It wouldn't. But a pair of socks would.'

\* \* \*

HUBBY      More money! Good gracious! I thought you had bought everybody a Christmas present.

WIFE  I thought I had too. But I've decided that most of them are too nice to give away.

\* \* \*

'I think that cooking is woman's work,' said the young wife. 'Yes,' replied her husband, pushing away his share of the Christmas turkey, 'and I have heard that a woman's work is never done.'

### Christmas in a Somerset Hospital, 1937 – extracts from a report in the *Devon and Somerset News*

There were twelve patients at Wellington Hospital for Christmas, and thanks to the unsparing efforts of the Matron and staff, all had a very happy time. The wards were tastefully decorated; in the women's ward a gay Christmas tree looked very attractive with its dainty canopy, and the beds were alternately treated with laburnum and wisteria.

On Christmas Day, visitors were permitted all day and each patient was allowed to invite two visitors to tea. In the evening there was some carol singing, with Miss W. Wyatt at the organ, and a delightful play 'The Bathroom Door', performed by members of the staff, was greatly enjoyed.

At 5.45 p.m. 'Father Christmas' paid a visit and presented each patient with a gift from the tree. At the call of the Matron hearty cheers were given for 'Father Christmas' and Miss Wyatt. In the course of the day visits were paid by Mr F. Hugh Fox, Miss Sully and Mr T.H. Richards, chairman and members of the Hospital committee, and Mr F. Lee-Mitchell, secretary.

Fifty-three children who had been patients in the course of the year accepted the Matron's invitation to a party on Boxing Day. As no beds were occupied in the men's ward, that room was ultilised for tea, for which a bountiful supply of tempting fare appeared on the tables. After tea, games and cards were enjoyed.

# · A West Country Christmas ·

**Remembering the Lads in the Forces – Wartime Christmas, 1939. Extract from the** *Marazion and Porthleven Advertiser*, **16 December 1939**

Those serving in HM Forces from Porthleven will not be forgotten this Christmastide. Already parcels are on the way to those distant men who unfortunately will not be able to spend the festive season at home with their loved ones.

The Women's Institute has forwarded a little Xmas gift to all who have entered the services.

For some time now members of the Women's Section of the British Legion have been busily preparing parcels. This week between 70 and 80 parcels containing cigarettes, magazines, chocolates to the value of 4s. a parcel have been dispatched.

The two Methodist Societies at Porthleven have also been engaged in parcel making. Their first intention of sending to their own members only was dropped and they extended their effort to cover all those who were away from Porthleven. On Wednesday they sent off 70 parcels containing 2s. 6d. worth of cigarettes and confectionery.

The vicar had previously sent to all the men from the Parish cigarettes etc. and written to each one individually.

**Christmas 1940. When the Colonel had a wooden horse from Santa Claus and six sergeants drank from a baby's bottle**

On Christmas night 1940, the YMCA entertained gunners and others to a party at an army camp somewhere in Somerset. Exactly where in the county it took place could not be mentioned in the newspapers because of wartime censorship. The following is an abridged version of an account which appeared in the next week's *Pulman's Weekly News* under the heading, 'A YMCA CAMP PARTY by One of the Guests':

*149*

# · *A West Country Christmas* ·

An excellent supper, an orchestra, games and competitions, charades, community singing, dancing, holly and mistletoe, a Christmas tree, and Santa Claus made it a real Christmas night for the soldiers spending their first Christmas in the army, their first perhaps away from home.

After being welcomed by Mr R.A. Hockeridge, leader of the hut, the guests sat down to supper which included Christmas pudding. During the dinner the Camp band played.

When cigarettes had been handed to each guest, all took part in community singing to the music of the band, led by Gunner A.V. George. Rousing cheers followed for the YMCA and the Commanding Officer expressed gratitude for its wonderful efforts.

Father Christmas appeared in traditional garb and carrying a full sack. His first present was for the Colonel – a wooden model of a horse, which the Colonel wheeled along the floor to the delight of everyone.

Father Christmas drew from his sack presents for every guest – books, writing materials, razor blades and other gifts.

Major Webster sang 'Four and Twenty Blackbirds' with appropriate actions; Gunner A.W. Rose gave a magical display; Private McKinnon, lightning caricatures and Gunner Noble a Spanish dance.

Competitions were held, the most popular being that to determine which of the six sergeants could drink with the greatest speed from a baby's bottle! It was won by Sergeant Cole.

A star turn was a charade on the word 'Bomb-ar-dier' arranged by Mrs R. Crowson and Miss Y. Cornish.

The rest of the evening was spent in competitions, ingenious versions of the old-fashioned musical chairs, and dancing to the band and the accordion played with great skill by Gunner A.L. Smith.

Finally at midnight, all sang 'Auld Lang Syne' and gave further cheers for the YMCA.

## Mother Dances with Santa Claus, 1949

'I saw Mummy kissing Santa Claus' was the title of a seasonal popular song a few years ago, but in Camborne in Cornwall in 1949, it was news when a mother danced with Santa Claus.

The report of the annual dinner of the Camborne Old Folk's Club in the Cornish newspaper, the *West Briton* on 15 December 1949, included the following paragraph:

> Canon C.H.S. Buckley (vicar of Gulval) dressed as Father Christmas, distributed gifts of fruits and sweets, and danced with 81 year old Mrs Mundy, who is the mother of 20 children.

And why shouldn't Mrs Mundy give Father Christmas the pleasure of a dance? After all, with stockings for all those children to be filled she'd kept Santa pretty busy over the years!

## The Days of Fairyland

For the boys and girls of Devon, a 'must' at Christmas time used to be a visit to 'Fairyland' at Waltons departmental store in Exeter – even if it meant, as it often did (especially on Saturdays), having to queue for a time to get in. Every year, for at least three decades, part of the store would be converted into a magical wonderland. Wide-eyed youngsters and their parents, having handed over their few pence, which went to charity, would wander through a world of make-believe – tableaux of nursery rhymes or scenes from favourite children's stories. And at the end, Father Christmas would be waiting with his able assistant, the Fairy Queen, to ask that familiar question – 'And what would you like for Christmas?'

stories. And at the end, Father Christmas would be waiting with his able assistant, the Fairy Queen, to ask that familiar question – 'And what would you like for Christmas?'

Between 1919 and 1949 a total of £12,294, the proceeds of Waltons 'Christmas Fairyland', was distributed to hospitals and charities. And between 1936 and 1949, there were over half a million visitors to 'Fairyland' – 262,611 children and 240,787 adults – which shows the appeal not only to the young, but also to the young at heart.

These statistics appeared in *The Shopping News*, 1950, a six-page, quarto-sized mock newspaper issued by Waltons. Besides providing details about 'Fairyland' and making a number of gift suggestions, the *News* contained two pages about the store's Toy Fair. Among the items mentioned as being available were dolls at prices from 2s. 6d. to £4, doll's houses 39s. 6d. to £7 15s. 3d., doll's prams 24s. 3d. to £10, soft toys from 6s. 8d. to £3, Meccano 7s. 3d. to 210s., Dinky Toys 9d. to 5s. 9d. and Christmas crackers from 3s. 6d. It also stated that Hornby trains were 'still in limited supply', and that, 'Waltons regret to say that our stocks will not last long but at the time of going to press we have our quota, with acccessories.'

The stop-press column of *The Shopping News*, for Christmas 1950, gave what was the latest position, at the time of going to press, of 'The Nylon Situation' – the stockings which were almost certainly *not* hung up for Father Christmas to fill!


## Lifeboat Tragedy, 1956

News of a tragedy involving the crew of a lifeboat, those brave men who risk their lives for others, is always heart-rending. When such an occurrence happens at Christmas time, it is particularly poignant.

# · *A West Country Christmas* ·

## A PAGE FOR THE *Kiddies*

## Here I am

# MEET ME

AT *Waltons*

# FAIRYLAND

YOU KNOW THE ENTRANCE
IS IN GOLDSMITH STREET

Bring your 3d. which will go to some charity, with all the other threepences. The grown-ups bring fourpence.

**The CHRISTMAS STORE**

# · *A West Country Christmas* ·

Around tea-time on Christmas Day in 1956, the crew of the Exmouth lifeboat *Maria Noble* were by their firesides enjoying the Christmas celebrations with their friends, relations and families. Little did they know what fate held in store for them, and what was facing them when the maroons summoned them to duty just before 5 p.m. For one of their number it was to be a call to his death.

The *Exmouth Journal* of 29 December 1956 described how the *Maria Noble* was launched in a full south-easterly gale to go to the aid of the *Minerva*, a 300-ton vessel which had sent up a distress signal about four miles offshore. As the lifeboat ploughed through heavy seas, in what the paper described as 'the wildest and stormiest Christmas Day of the town's history', two of the crew – Bill Carder and second coxswain Jack Phillips – were washed overboard. The *Journal*'s report went on: 'Nobody believed there was the slightest hope for the two missing men. All who knew something of the conditions were only too well aware that only a miracle could save them. There was, of course, the bare possibility that the south-easterly gale would drive them on to the beach on the Exmouth side of Straight Point, but that either would be alive was just too much to hope for.'

The miracle almost happened, however. The two were washed ashore, where they were found by search parties organized after news of the accident had been received by radio from the lifeboat. Jack Phillips was found first, completely exhausted, and, after being given first aid on the beach, he was rushed to hospital where he subsequently recovered. But for Bill Carder, it was too late. His body was discovered shortly afterwards, laying face down in he surf. All efforts to revive him failed and that Christmas of 1956 was his last.

*from*

# In the Country

## KENNETH ALLSOP

*From Christmas 'as it used to be', let's turn now to a more contemporary look at the festival with some more West Country writers. Kenneth Allsop was well known as both a journalist and broadcaster in the 1960s and early '70s. He worked on both the* Sunday Times *and the* Evening Standard *as well as working as literary editor on the* Daily Mail. *He was also well known for his appearances on BBC Television as both an interviewer and commentator. Sadly, and prematurely, Kenneth Allsop died in 1973.*

*This extract comes from* In the Country, *published in 1972. The book was compiled from a journal that he kept (and which formed the basis of a series of articles for the* Daily Mail) *when he moved from London to live in a Dorset mill-house.*

On a sycamore's highest twig a strapping bird, marked like a leopard in front, is raking the dripping valley with loud screaking notes.

I hurry, log under arm, from the coppice. The air wraps around me like a wet bandage. The Knoll, the far ridge, the beech wood are all a faded sepia photograph, outlines almost

erased. Uncheered by the mistle thrush's banshee song, I am anxious to get indoors, out of the short day already at its last gasp.

I enter the house where cacti droop in a fetid little conservatory. Living in my house has the feeling of being in a railway train shunted up a siding, for it is long and skinny with windows each side of the compartment rooms.

At one end is what could pass for Stephenson's *Rocket*: all those curly black pipes, iron wheels and knobby bolts of the slumbering turbines in the mill-room. By passing from there through an interminable series of doors (down the length of the unswaying carriages) you eventually reach the dining-car.

Here the Aga throbs with heat. Dogs stretch nose-to-tail all the way under the ovens, melting the marrow of their backbones. One stage farther is the pantry, big as a guard's van, with cool slate shelves and whopping ceiling hooks where the hams hung.

The kitchen is where the gang hangs out. It is my favourite place. Earlier I was sidling down from my office to wring out a third cup of tea and palm another steaming mince pie from the wire tray. It is more than usually cluttered. The Welsh dresser is just normally piled like a rummage sale, with pliers, copies of *Mad*, pebbles from the beach, a paintbrush, the Parish Mag and some dried artichokes. Amid muddy gumboots the Windsor chair is invisible under duffle-coats and Afghan cloaks: a memorial mound to my twenty years of failure to get clothing hung up in cupboards.

The long elm table in the centre of the tiled floor is like a lost property counter. Unemptied shopping bags spill figs and paper parcels; unopened magazines are piled with boxes of moth-eaten decorations brought down from the attic yet again.

One son is eating what appears to be a large breakfast; the other has decided that a drink is due, and is sampling the rum

which my wife is mixing into a sauce. Snatches of disjointed chat and urgent instructions occasionally beat the record player in volume. The butcher calls. The telephone rings. The kettle whistles. The dogs bark.

I have lost contact with reality. Beyond the glass door the garden waves greyly and dreamlike, and a robin perches on a tub, a small glowing bulb in the creeping twilight.

There is a sense of high vibrations mounting to the point where reason snaps and erratic behaviour may break out. My daughter, spraying tracer fire of purple cream from a metal gun, is writing on a cake's white icing: 'Merry Christmas to all Our Readers.'

I am beginning to suspect that something is afoot.

My children headed homeward from art school in the far north, from university two hundred miles east, from first job in the west. They converged upon this southerly base with a clatter of rusted wings and the throb of ruptured silencers.

How nice it is in the turmoil of eleventh-hour shopping and furtive present-wrapping, to have them gathered together for Christmas. They will be able to deal with the cutting of the holly. I felt that my lily white hands weren't up to such rough stuff.

I know where the scratchy sprigs can be got. I have had my eye on that tree. It stands in the wild hedge beside the stile at the foot of Round Knoll.

It is a fine mature forty-five foot stalwart with a girth like a bull's – hollies grow big down here in the humid mildness. But until October I had not been sure if we could crop it for household decoration.

You can't tell with a holly. It may turn out to be the wrong sex. Some people are unreasonably resentful because, although their holly has creamy blooms in May, it doesn't generate a single spark of fruit.

They ask too much of it. They own a male whose business is

dusting honey bees with yellow pollen, with which the flowers of a female tree – hopefully within whistling distance – can be fertilised.

We are lucky. Our holly is a precious she-tree. Its shellacked leaves glint in the pale, malt whisky wash of the winter sun. And its berries are as brilliant as fairylights. It is a ready-made Christmas tree.

Apprehensively I had watched the chattering autumn flocks of fieldfares – strapping, gaudy thrushes from Scandinavia – looting along the hedgerow and gulping berries like peanuts at a drinks party.

The clusters are so profuse that you can't see where their beaks dug in. There is enough for all.

So off through the frost-crackling mud my children and their friends went to bring back the bounty, and I made for the coppice to see about that trunk section I had ear-marked as being a likely looking Yule log when I had been picking up the lighter stuff. Sloshing through the pulpy leaves I came to it. Just what we needed. That would have roasting flames roaring up the chimney. But it was lacking one minor essential: a horse team and chains. Perhaps I should have dished out the tasks differently, seen to the holly myself and left the hauling of the log to all those restless young muscles.

I slunk back to the house and applied myself to the urgent labour of reading a review book at the fireside. It was considerate of me, I decided, to let the children get the holly. And they sorted it out in the crowded kitchen, plaiting a garland for the brass knocker and hanging it over the fire's cross beam, they would be enacting fun and mystery as perennial as 'the rising of the sun and the running of the deer'.

# · *A West Country Christmas* ·

The North Devon town of Ilfracombe in the snow in 1940

159

# Christmas Card

## TED HUGHES

*The current Poet Laureate, Ted Hughes, now lives and writes in North Devon. Here is his seasonal offering.*

You have anti-freeze in the car, yes,
And the shivering stars wade deeper,
Your scarf's tucked in under your buttons,
But a dry snow ticks through the stubble.
Your knee-boots gleam in the fashion,
But the moon must stay

    And stamp and cry
    As the holly the holly
    Hots its reds.

Electric blanket to comfort your bedtime
The river no longer feels its stones.
Your windows are steamed by dumpling laughter
The snowplough's buried on the drifted moor.
Carols shake your television
And nothing moves on the road but the wind

    Hither and thither
    The wind and three
    Starving sheep.

# · A West Country Christmas ·

Redwings from Norway rattle at the clouds
And comfortless sneezers puddle in pubs.
The robin looks in at the kitchen window
And all care huddles to hearths and kettles.
The sun lobs one wet snowball feebly
Brim and blue

    The dusk of the combe
    And the swamp woodland
    Sinks with the wren.

See old lips go purple and old brows go paler
The stiff cow drops in the midnight silence.
Sneezes grow coughs and coughs grow painful.
The vixen yells in the midnight garden.
You wake with the shakes and watch your breathing
Smoke in the moonlight – silent, silent.

    Your anklebone
    And your anklebone
    Lie big in your bed.

# A Collection of
# Christmas Goodies

## ARTHUR MARSHALL

*Arthur Marshall will of course be known to millions of viewers of the extremely popular BBC Television series,* Call My Bluff, *when every week he and his colleagues pitted their wits and verbal skills against Frank Muir and his team. I had been hoping to interview Arthur Marshall for an* In Conversation *programme for the BBC but sadly he fell ill, and died early in 1989, so we never met. He lived at Christow, a small village near Exeter and I am very grateful to his friend Peter Kelland for pointing me in the direction of the following piece which is a combination of several articles that Arthur Marshall wrote for the* New Statesman *magazine (now the* New Statesman and Society) *between 1976 and 1981. Reading these words, one can almost hear Arthur's voice again, that lazy, languid almost superior delivery with the ever present note of mischief not far off – he will be greatly missed.*

One only hopes that this year not a single penny of public money is going to be wasted on street displays of illuminated and sodden Santas idiotically beaming. One's mind flies back to the days long ago when the percentage of church-goers was

very much higher and the general expenditure on tinselly rubbish considerably lower.

In the 1920s and '30s very few Christmas cards were sent and in general limited to family ones. Some now prefer to insert news of their intentions in the personal columns of papers and I admire those strong willed enough to announce to the world that 'Nibs and Bimbo Ointment are sending no cards this year and are subscribing instead to the NSPCC.'

The Bultitudes' elaborate 'personalised' Christmas card, specially printed at Heavens knows what cost, has arrived ('Cordially yours, Bunty and Giles') and has irritated almost everybody.

Many of the cards that one gets fill one with either guilt (no Christmas *quid pro quo* from me to them) or a feeling of inadequacy (that 45p incompletely erased on the back reveals their lavish expenditure, far in excess of one's own 8p). Absence of cards from old chums greatly worried my mother and for days after the event she could be heard muttering things such as 'I simply can't think why I haven't heard from Hilda Desborough.'

One year we found ourselves caught rather on the hop (no mince-pies ready and no hot drinks) by the arrival, a day earlier than usual, of the church carol singers, twenty strong and complete with lanterns and pink cheeks and a tuneful descant for the final verse of 'O Come all Ye Faithful'. However a rustling banknote of relatively handsome dimensions cheered everybody up and they exited from the garden on a wave of *bonhomie* and good will. (Mrs Entwhistle, the soul of kindess and hospitality is said to have been experimenting with hot punch for visitors and has already rendered four child carol singers – two hurried verses of 'Good King Wenceslas' and then ring the bell – almost insensible with alcohol.)

Plans for the 'Over 75s' Yuletide Feast are well ahead (it was to have been 'Over 70s' but their number was found to be far

too excessive for the capacities of the village hall — a real feather in the cap of the National Health Service) and should there be a wintry cold snap, here's a handy hint for the elderly and others. I am reliably informed that the body's maximum heat loss occurs through the head which is, after all, totally unprotected and exposed. Therefore pop on a warmish hat indoors and never mind how dotty you look siting there. This has an added advantage. Uninvited, and almost certainly unwanted, chance callers at the house, heralded by that dread cry of 'Anybody home?' from the garden path, will spot your headpiece and will invariably jump to the wrong conclusion. 'Oh, I see you're just going out.') You'll be rid of them in two minutes.

The Christmas feast to which I have referred will be run and prepared and cooked and supervised by some of those splendid, large solid and motherly women who flourish so abundantly in villages. They only truly feel at home behind a large teapot. They man, if that be the verb, the Women's Institutes and Mother's Unions, they deliver the meals on wheels ('How are we today?'), they get up sales of work in aid of repairs to the hall and even the venerable church roof (You'd think that the Maker would at least look after His property), they make cakes and jams, they visit the sick and they are ready to do any kind and useful deed. They are, thank goodness, imperishable. One generation of them gives birth to another and on and on they go. They do not dabble in commercial affairs but of course such cheerful and efficient people would really be the only hope of improvement in those motorway eating places which are mostly caverns of gloom and appallingly expensive at that. Two really competent and experienced village housewives, horrified at soggy toast, limp bacon, deeply unattractive 'coffee vending machines', grubby table tops and the suicidal looks on the faces of most of those dispensing the unappealing eatables, would have everything to rights in a jiffy. The only

Arthur Marshall

165

coffee vending machine that they understand is a large smiling lady with a jug.

With Christmas comes the exchange of geriatric gifts – a hot water bottle here, a pair of hand-knitted mittens there – and the Bultitudes' cheerfully indiscriminate and blanket hospitality ('Crash on up any time for a noggin'), warming and delighting everybody. It is clear that Bunty's new hair arrangement (a sort of mini-Tower of Pisa embellished with diamanté combs) will be quite a little talking point in the village for some time to come. Even Mrs Entwhistle, herself a pioneer and always one to welcome either a sartorial or corporal novelty in others, was visibly taken aback, though Giles of course ('Doesn't the old girl look a treat') was his usual loyal self.

Bultitude champagne flowed throughout the season (Canon and Mrs Mountjoy were each seen to lower three glasses and to do full justice to the cocktail-stick-skewered chipolatas) and two no kinder persons than the Colonel and his consort ever lived. So who minds the occasional shrieks of 'Bottoms up, chaps!' and 'Cheerybung!' and lavatory doors labelled 'HERE IT IS'?

You'll probably want to know about our Christmas lunch. There were seven 'couverts' and when I tell you in all honesty, that the average age of those present was 78, and that I was the youngest but one, you will see how defiantly game we all are down here. My cousin Madge, now nudging ninety, made a resplendent and distinguished figure upon my right and commented favourably upon my unusual table decoration – sprigs of witch-hazel and yellow jasmine, both currently in full flower combined with the lightish green holly with yellow trimmed leaves, the three concomitants forming really quite a pleasing and happy ensemble; do feel free to copy it.

Although no formal grace was said before we ate, the more thoughtful amongst us offered up a silent and heartfelt word of

thanks not to the Almighty but to Messrs Marks and Spencer, to whom we owed, not in a financial sense, the nine pound turkey, the spuds, the sprouts, the sausages, the bacon rolls and when it came, the Christmas pudding, all of them purchased in a pre-Christmas press of humanity, which, although one risked being trampled underfoot, greatly cheered those of us who chance to be shareholders.

Opinions about the cooking of poultry differ, and those that tell you that one and a quarter hours is sufficient roasting-time for a medium sized chicken are talking through their hats, but our turkey responded nobly and admirably to three hours, starting breast down at 375° whatever they are, with the heat very gradually reduced and the bird, now right side up, moving like some giant theatre star on the skids, ever lower in the oven and landing up on the bottom where it 'rested' for a space, encircled with roast potatoes and sausages and the very picture of tender deliciousness.

Opinions about menus differ too and in my view it is inadvisable to have anything at all before a turkey, a bucket of soup or some savory and cheesy fish thing being quite unnecessary and ruining everybody's full appreciation of the main *plat*. Although I know that electric carving knives exist, I myself carve with the small-toothed side of a serrated bread-knife (no risk of tearing the flesh) and I noticed no dissatisfaction or glum faces. The Christmas pudding steamed for four hours, was perfection, with mince pies and Devonshire cream completing what some were kind enough to refer to, though not in those precise terms, as a gourmet's dream, a view with which I cannot honestly concur, for both the bread sauce and the turkey stuffing were from a packet, admirable though the results were. Mrs Beeton, not to speak of my mother or two grandmothers, would have had fifty fits, one or other of the latter possibly swooning dead away. But oh my goodness, the convenience of a packet, eh what?

# · A West Country Christmas ·

You are probably anxiously wondering what was offered in the way of liquid refreshment and here taste and refinement went hand in hand. There were three different kinds of sherry, dry, less dry and not at all dry. There were assorted spirits, for those that find that they absolutely must. My cousin Madge's internal arrangements require her to drink white wine rather than red, but with our lunch the rest of us drank a claret that boldly announced itself on the bottle as being 'CLARET', adding that it was 'famed for its elegance' and 'the traditional accompaniment to game and roasts'. It was shipped and bottled by a firm established since 1769 and in the entirely reputable area of London called St James, and any firm that has remained for over two hundred years in SW1 is alright with me.

I was deeply attached to my Devon grandmother, a lovely circular giggler who took little, except her religion and good deeds seriously and with whom we spent most of my youthful Christmases. By the time the festive evening arrived, it had already been an exhausting day for her. She had of course, attended Holy Communion, together with all the other adults in the house apart from my Uncle Oswald, a firm disbeliever and provider of ribald jokes ('How was the wine?') at the breakfast table.

At Christmas dinner, and seated near her, I used to watch with some anxiety the changing colours on her face. Although high blood is by no means always revealed in a flourid complexion, my dear grandmother went in for colour. Her pressure was said to be the highest in the county and was even rumoured to have broken, during a test, Dr Bentley's apparatus, though the fact came from my Uncle Oswald previously shown to be a mischievous and not always trustworthy informant. In her case the damaging pressure showed itself in her cheeks, now crimson, now mauve and settling finally, as her share of the succulent goodies disappeared, for a disturbing purple. I would like to report that mindful of Dr Bentley's

# · A West Country Christmas ·

Bringing in the Christmas pudding to a Victorian table

warnings, not to speak of his bust contraption, she ate prudently and frugally but the truth obliges me to say that she simply gobbled it all down. The word 'shovel' used as a verb neatly sums up her deft work with fork, knife and spoon. The menu was unvarying. There was turtle soup. There was fish, for to the Victorian that my grandmother was, no dinner was a dinner without it. There was The Bird, stuffed with all the necessary and numerous concomitants. Then the lights were momentarily extinguished and my grandmother's parlour maid, Emma, proudly brought in to cries of 'Oooh!' the Christmas pudding, fully alight. There were mince pies. There was Stilton. There was coffee and port and tangerines and chocs and Brazil nuts and a vast assortment of crystallised fruits, merely pecked at, so full were we, and which lingered on for weeks in an increasingly sticky and displeasing mass.

Those who have by now become revolted by this recital of what to many may seem greed and gluttony can cheer up on receiving the assurance that such fare is purely seasonal and that, when the final devilled turkey leg has gone down the red lane, we shall go back to our regular and humble round of kippers and stews and toad-in-the-hole.

As there were children present, there were, of course, crackers which were considered to be an indispensably merry part of the proceedings. They looked, dotted about the table and with at least one within easy reach, very jolly and attractive (difficult to construct an ugly cracker for its shape alone is agreeable and inviting). They contained, as usual, paper hats, none of which ever suited my grandmother and made her look like Napoleon on a bad day and a rather raffish pirate or a member of the French Revolution *en route* for Versailles with a grievance. Sometimes there was an exciting box of indoor fireworks, for the enjoyment of which Emma brought in a large tin tray on which the various combustibles could be set off and for which, the better to see them, the room lights were extinguished. There were magnesium flares which sparkled prettily in a twinkling star pattern. There were paper balloons which burst into flames as dramatically as the Hindenberg and then miraculously lifted themselves off the tray and sailed, in blackened ruins, to the ceiling and, after a bit, descended and usually on to something unfortunate – my father's immaculately starched shirt or my aunt's chevelure or, indeed, the crystallised fruits. There were ('IGNITE AND STAND WELL BACK') coloured pictures of some shooting or other, often a bearded Westerner picking off a Red Indian, and a large X at the rifle tip showed where a glowing match end must be applied, upon which, and with much spluttering and crackling, a line of fire extended from the gun to the fleeing native and reached him with a loud explosion. For these things, my grandmother had her fingers in her ears ('Just tell me when it's over, darling') and wore on her mottled face an expression of intense suffering, probably not so much for the victim's demise as the din of his passing. And sometimes, though these were usually in the crackers, there were Japanese water flowers, which looked, being tightly folded rolls of paper, unpromising, but which, laid on the surface of a glass of water, gradually unfolded themselves into entrancing flower shapes and colours.

Those readers who are sniffing slightly in disapproval and are thinking that we all made pigs of ourselves are quite correct. We did. Should we have been thinking of the starving multitudes elewhere? Yes we should. Were we? No we weren't.

# Thoughts of Christmas

## BLANCHE MUDGE

*This is another poem from* A West Country New Anthology of Contemporary Poets. *Blanche Mudge seems to have been a Victorian writer, though I have been unable to find out anything more about her. Her poem turns from a feeling of sadness amongst the festive joy to end on an optimistic, almost triumphant, note. It seems to*

# · *A West Country Christmas* ·

*me to be the perfect way to end this collection and celebration of* A West Country Christmas.

Sad are the dreams of solitude,
The crowded memories that intrude
Midst Yuletide's glad beatitude.

No little feet with pattering tread
Ran up the nursery stairs to bed;
I miss each silken, curly head.

The merry voices clear and bright
Whose laughter rang from morn till night
In one long rapture of delight.

On Christmas Eve I lay at rest,
Still mourning for my empty nest,
And all my griefs were soothed and blest.

Into the chamber where I slept,
A little child in secret crept,
A helpless, tender Babe, who wept.

At my heart's door He pleading cried,
'There is no room for Me outside,'
Gladly my heart I opened wide.

Adoring that sweet Infant face,
I made for him a dwelling place,
Where he abides a little space.

No longer were my heart strings torn:
Great joy was mine on Christmas morn
Because that little Babe was born.

All Christmas joy be yours.

# Acknowledgements

My grateful thanks to my wife, Lucy, for her patience with a man who celebrated Christmas early in our household in front of a green-eyed monster called a word processor. Thanks are also due to the following for their invaluable help in compiling this book:

All the staff at the West Country Studies Library and the Central Library in Exeter for their tolerance with a research novice; Revd Patrick Riley; John Brunsdon; George Pridmore; Robin Stanes; John Somers; Edwin G. Crook; Lionel Woodley; Peter Kelland; Wendy Logan for 'baby sitting'; Chris Robinson; Lawrence Daeche; John Saunders at Exeter University; and most of all my brother Paul, for setting me off firmly in the right direction.

'Angel's Song' from *Gift From a Lamb* by Charles Causley is reprinted by permission of Robson Books Ltd; 'The Legend of Penrose' from *Vanishing Cornwall* by Daphne du Maurier, by permission of Christian Browning; the extract from *Hercule Poirot's Christmas* by Agatha Christie, by permission of Brian Stone of Aitken & Stone Ltd; 'The Yule Log' from *Linhay on the Downs* by Henry Williamson, by permission of Anne Williamson and the Henry Williamson Literary Estate; 'A Devon Country Christmas', by permission of BBC Radio Devon; the extract from *In the Country* by Kenneth Allsop, by permission of the Peters Fraser and Dunlop Group Ltd; 'Christmas Card' from *Season Songs* by Ted Hughes, by permission of Faber and Faber Ltd; and 'Christmas Goodies' by Arthur Marshall, by kind permission of the *New Statesman and Society*.

# Picture credits

Steve Bower, p. 2; BBC Radio Devon, p. 120; Chris Chapman, pp. 69, 113; The Clovelly Collection, Sheila Ellis, pp. 52, 54; *Cornish Evening Tidings*, p. 146; The Edwin G. Crook Collection, pp. i, 5, 9, 13, 65, 161, 173; Dorset Natural History and Archaeological Society, Dorset County Museum, Dorchester, Dorset, p. 91; Mary Evans Picture Library, pp. 34, 87, 169; *Express and Echo*, Exeter, pp. 28, 133; Ilfracombe Museum Collection, pp. 22, 123, 127, 159; *Illustrated Western Weekly News*, pp. 43, 84; Peter Kelland, p. 165; Frank Lavin, p. 107; Terry Linee, p. 37; London Weekend Television, p. 102; The Stanley MacKenzie Collection, p. 71; Jim Manson, p. 61; John Morland, p. 75; The Post Office, p. 77; James Ravilious, p. 18; June Smith, p. 117; Taunton Cider Company, p. 41; Brian Walker, p. 76; *The Waltons Shopping News*, p. 153; George Weidenfeld & Nicolson Ltd, p. 20; Lionel Woodley, p. 45.